FROM
ORDINARY to
AWESOME

A POSITIVE
ACTION
CHALLENGE
FOR YOUR
TRANSFORMATION -
A JOURNAL

RENEE M **SHALHOUB**

BALBOA.PRESS
A DIVISION OF HAY HOUSE

Balboa Press books may be ordered through booksellers or by contacting:

Balboa Press
A Division of Hay House
1663 Liberty Drive
Bloomington, IN 47403
www.balboapress.com
1 (877) 407-4847

Because of the dynamic nature of the Internet, any web addresses or links contained in this book may have changed since publication and may no longer be valid. The views expressed in this work are solely those of the author and do not necessarily reflect the views of the publisher, and the publisher hereby disclaims any responsibility for them.

The author of this book does not dispense medical advice or prescribe the use of any technique as a form of treatment for physical, emotional, or medical problems without the advice of a physician, either directly or indirectly. The intent of the author is only to offer information of a general nature to help you in your quest for emotional and spiritual well-being. In the event you use any of the information in this book for yourself, which is your constitutional right, the author and the publisher assume no responsibility for your actions.

Any people depicted in stock imagery provided by Getty Images are models, and such images are being used for illustrative purposes only.
Certain stock imagery © Getty Images.

Print information available on the last page.

Scripture marked (KJV) taken from the King James Version of the Bible. Scripture quotations marked (TLB) are taken from The Living Bible copyright © 1971. Used by permission of Tyndale House Publishers, a Division of Tyndale House Ministries, Carol Stream, Illinois 60188. All rights reserved.

ISBN: 978-1-9822-3877-3 (sc)
ISBN: 978-1-9822-3878-0 (e)

Balboa Press rev. date: 05/22/2020

To my daughter, Jacqueline Kelly, who inspires me every day to be a better person and without whom many of my ideas and passions for life would lie dormant.

If you want to awaken all of humanity, then awaken all of yourself. If you want to eliminate the suffering in the world, then eliminate all that is dark and negative in yourself.
Truly, the greatest gift you have to give is that of your own self-transformation.

—Lao Tzu

TAKE ACTION!

Are you Up for the Challenge of Transforming your Life?

Positive Action Challenge
will inspire and excite you!

FOLLOW ONE THEME EACH WEEK.

ACCEPT THE CHALLENGE.

CHANGE YOUR LIFE!

CONTENTS

PREFACE

Who knew that what started out as a game on one cloudy and boring Mother's Day afternoon would turn into a two-year weekly practice of writing a motivational blog? Not this hesitant author; that's for sure!

I simply wanted to inspire my daughter, myself, and a few family members to take action to make our lives more kind, more interactive, more introspective, and more *more*!

More what specifically, you might ask? More is whatever you want it to be. More is up for interpretation based on what you define as a happy life:

> What makes you happy?
> What makes you feel good about yourself?
> What makes you the best you can be?
> What stops you from being your best self?

The first challenge that I remember challenging my daughter and family to do was to "smile at five strangers and try to make them smile back at you." Simple really, but it isn't an easy task for a person who is unaccustomed to looking at strangers in the eye and smiling in the first place. Looking at someone who is a stranger and smiling at them is out of many people's comfort zones especially since many of us tend to look down or bury our eyes in our cell phones. However, the idea of each section of this book is to challenge ourselves to be better. To change ourselves in some small way to rise above our fears and inhibitions and become the best version of ourselves.

What I want—no, what I *need*—readers to know is that the content and format of this book may sometimes seem odd or awkward because it was originally written in the form of emails, which I sent out to six family members. Those family members liked what they read and enjoyed the challenges. So, with their encouragement and further brainstorming, I gathered twelve friends as a test group and attempted a trial run of writing a blog.

I enjoyed writing the blog so much that I continued it and expanded it for a couple of years! I started out writing five days a week, which became overwhelming and decided that writing three days every week worked out better for everyone. I enjoyed the writing, and my readers seemed to enjoy the receiving.

Taking an electronic version of writing and transcribing it into a print version doesn't always easily transfer. I sometimes refer to holidays and or family members because I wrote blog entries every week over the course of two years and, therefore, I recognize a holiday, a birthday, and/or an anniversary here and there.

While I initially began the journey of creating challenges for others, I found that the more I wrote, the more I traveled inward, searching my own soul, my own past, and my own heart. My challenges and musing were not only for others but became for myself and for the development of my own character and for my own true-self to blossom into what I know myself to be—a fully independent person. The things that have thwarted my success on the road to becoming who I am, may just happen to have an effect on many others as well. So, my writings, albeit cathartic, I pray, may be helpful to someone else along the way.

ACKNOWLEDGMENTS

Thank you. Thank you. Thank you.

It would have been impossible to write this book without the support and love of my family and friends.

So much gratitude to my husband, Al, for his patience, love, and guidance, especially during times of my frustration and writer's block; for his inspiration and love; and for his written contribution.

Thank you to my son Shane for all the many lengthy conversations of encouragement; for his feedback, support, and understanding; and for getting all of his friends excited to read my message.

To my daughter-in-law, Christina, go my thanks for her unyielding support, encouragement, and meaningful conversations and for her written contribution. And to my son Dan go my thanks for his support and guidance and positive attitude. Thank you to my son Greg for his love.

My gratitude to my friend Patty for her patience; love; and many long, insightful conversations.

Thank you to my friend Karen for her technological support and guidance in order to start blogging in the first place, as I am definitely challenged in the world of computers.

To my new friends Sandy and Brooke, who helped to keep me focused on completion, thank you.

The encouragement and support and feedback and comments of the original twelve members of the blog are greatly appreciated. And while I may not mention you all by name, you know who you are, and I send love and gratitude to you all.

INTRODUCTION

Grab this book, a blank notebook or journal, and a pen and set off on your personal journey toward transformation!

Be prepared for reflection, as each *Positive Action Challenge for Your Transformation* is meant to be savored over a period of time. Readers are encouraged to read one section each week - which contains three to five chapters – and journal either daily or weekly as thoughts of change and transformation occur.

While you are reading each weekly entry, it is strongly suggested that you, the reader, take the time to think about and reflect on each challenge and chapter. After all, each entry was written for a one-week reflection, and the book isn't meant to be read as a "quick read," like a novella or a short story. Ideally, your personal journal could be kept so that you might take note of your own journey of self-transformation.

Like many people who look to transform themselves, I wrote each of these sections and chapters on each character trait like a journal as it occurred pertinent in my life. In some cases, entries related to a season, such as generosity and giving pertain to the holidays and love relates to Valentine's Day. With others, it was simply that I was having an experience in my personal life at the time and I wanted and needed to write about it to explore how to become more fully evolved as a human being. Writing helps me to sort through my emotions, thoughts and feelings in more depth than just reading and thinking about it.

However, my opinion is that many people have a majority of the character traits listed here, if not all of them. And, if you're like me and hope to develop yourself to your fullest whole self, then you'll want to read each entry, either in the order that they are presented or in the order in which you see fit based on which character trait calls out to you and what you are dealing with in life at the present moment. Since, the sections of this book were first written as a blog on the internet they no longer fall in accord to the seasons and months of the calendar in which they were originally formatted they might sometimes seem out of context but that is due to the fact that they were written according to the calendar year originally.

As a former educator, I considered the best way to organize the contents of this book to be alphabetically. After all, each entry is a character trait that each of us has and might aspire to develop. Therefore, the easiest way to look up the character trait you want to focus on and read about would be in alphabetical order. However, the entries were not originally written in the order in which they are presented here.

Regardless of the order in which you read the content of the book; my goal is for you to read one-character trait per week. Reflect on whether or not you want to make a change in that area of your life, in an attempt to decide if you are doing enough to live life to your fullest potential. And ultimately, I hope that each and every one of you will transform every area of your character in the ways you see fit to strengthen your inner moral compass and live your lives completely with love, kindness, and prosperity.

Just as the writing of this book was cathartic for me, the journey through each weekly challenge can and may be cathartic for you. Therefore, my hope is that each reader not only find something for themselves through the reading of the passages but also discover more fully their true path in life through journaling.

What part of your life do you dream of transforming? Relationships? Work? Home? School? Life in general?

In what area of life are you willing to challenge yourself?

Which character trait are you willing to explore?

Willingness is the first step toward transforming your life. Are you willing to try? Are you willing to be open to new ideas? Are you willing to be open to old ideas presented differently?

It doesn't matter if you think you've tried to change in the past and failed. It doesn't matter if you think you might have a negative attitude.

You just have to be willing to try!

Suggested Journal Questions

Some suggested journal questions to answer as you read include:

1. What emotions do you experience as you read today's challenge?
2. How is this challenge difficult? How is this challenge easy?
3. What can I do to make this character trait better in myself? For myself? For others?
4. What is it about this character trait that I want to change?
5. What is it about this challenge that I do not want to do?
6. What is it about this challenge that I find confronting?
7. Do I want to keep this character trait exactly the way it is for my ultimate happiness?
8. What tools am I using to soothe my anxieties and stress?
9. Which tools work best for me?

Happy Reading
Happy Writing
To your Transformation !

CHAPTER 1

ACCEPTANCE

ACCEPTANCE #1

Acceptance doesn't mean resignation; it means understanding that something is what it is and that there's got to be a way through it.

—Michael J. Fox

Many things occur in our lives that challenge us—illness, separation, loss of income, rejection, foreclosure, death. It's difficult to be accepting during these difficult times, as our emotions are turbulent and often override our reason and sensibility. Our immediate reaction may be an emotional one, which is our natural human response. We might cry or strike out in anger.

> These years in silence and reflection made me stronger and reminded me that acceptance has to come from within and that this kind of truth gives me the power to conquer emotions I didn't even know existed. (Ricky Martin)

When our emotions settle down and we are able to think rationally, the next important step is to find a way toward acceptance.

I remember when I was diagnosed with a seizure disorder as an adult some years ago. My body was not working properly—that was clear—but

1

my mind was in total denial. I was sure that there was some serious error in the doctor's diagnosis. This couldn't be true. My brain couldn't be malfunctioning. I was frightened, scared, and angry. Up until this time, I had spent the first fifty years of my life illness free, active, and independent. I was lucky!

It took months for me to adjust to my new normal—life on medication that would control my seizures and some limited activities. What helped me adjust the most, however, was acceptance. I had to accept my condition and then adapt without hesitation or worry.

Your challenge is to move toward acceptance of what is!

How do you move toward acceptance? Be kind to yourself—love yourself as you would love a good friend. Forgive yourself. Celebrate your strengths. Create a support system. Allow yourself to grieve your loss. Do kind things for others—focusing on others will take your focus off yourself. Be grateful.

Self-acceptance is part of self-love. We must accept ourselves as we are in order to move forward.

To your transformation!

ACCEPTANCE #2

> *Acceptance looks like a passive state, but in reality, it brings something entirely new into this world. That peace, a subtle energy vibration, is consciousness.*
>
> —Eckhart Tolle

When you find that you have acceptance of what is, you will have a wave of peace that washes over you like a soft, invisible shroud.

Acceptance does not mean that you do not take action to change the things that you can change. Acceptance means that you quietly allow those things that you have no control over—those things you cannot change no matter how much action you take—to exist peacefully in your universe.

So, continue to do everything that you physically can do to make your life great. Do everything that you can do to make your life emotionally stable.

Continuing your best effort is always your challenge, as is accepting people and things as they are, those things that you cannot change, as you continue to do your best.

Once you are able to accept those things, you will have no worries. Worrying about those people or those events will not change anything. Worrying will only make you sick, both physically and emotionally.

Once you have done your best, you will be free—free from remorse, free from regret, and free to accept what is!

To your transformation!

> *The acceptance of certain realities doesn't preclude idealism.*
> *It can lead to certain breakthroughs.*
> —Rem Koolhaas

ACCEPTANCE #3

> *The ancient Greeks and Romans also held the view that*
> *acceptance is the beginning of wisdom.*
> —Simon Van Booy

Your acceptance of yourself is paramount to happiness, yet we all continue to seek acceptance by others.

If the others that we seek tend to reject us, it's important for us to accept those people for their limitations in their ability to accept us.

If you've done something to offend them and have apologized, that's all you can do. If you've created new possibilities for your life that other people cannot or will not see or accept, that's okay too.

You can only do your best. You can only *be* your best.

Look elsewhere for acceptance.

Look inside yourself for acceptance.

Accept those who do not accept you with love and understanding for who they are and for where they are.

Your acceptance will set you free.

To your freedom!

To your transformation!

I'm hopeful for a world with more love, acceptance, and compassion for others.

—Lily Alridge

CHAPTER 2
ACKNOWLEDGMENT*

By taking the time to stop and appreciate who you are and what you've achieved—and perhaps learned through a few mistakes, stumbles and losses—you actually can enhance everything about you. Self-acknowledgment and appreciation are what give you the insights and awareness to move forward toward higher goals and accomplishments.

—Jack Canfield

As I met more people and listen to their stories, I started recognizing that what pushes them are the things they care about. So I started thinking about what I care about and why I care about it.

I started with the big picture of people in my life and my work. Then I thought about the day-to-day items, such as why I cared so much about having a clean house or getting to work early. I realized that, when I care, I try harder!

I thought about what caring means and what my core values were. I recognized that my core values include accountability and leaving a place better than I found it.

Here's your challenge. This week, take time to ask yourself:

---

* Acknowledgement – all three entries were written by C. Garibian Asbaty

5

What do I care about?
Why do I care about those things?
And what are my core values?

See where there are gaps between what you care about and how you are currently living your life.

To your transformation!

> *We spend a lot of time in our heads but when we take time to connect our heads to our hearts and dig deeper into what we care about, we are able to not only appreciate the strides that we have made thus far, we also start to appreciate and acknowledge ourselves and others in our life more effectively.*
> —C. Garibian-Asbaty

ACKNOWLEDGMENT #2

> *Don't rely on someone else for your happiness and self-worth. Only you can be responsible for that. If you can't love and respect yourself—no one else will be able to make that happen. Accept who you are—completely; the good and the bad—and make changes as you see fit—not because you think someone else wants you to be different — (but because you want to be different)!*
> —Stacey Charter

While we may receive acknowledgement from others, our true happiness lies in self-recognition and self-acknowledgement.

There are no gender barriers in this category. While some men *do* find it easier to acknowledge their own achievements, both genders need daily recognition in their personal relationships, work arenas, and all categories of their lives.

Yet sometimes it's difficult for us to see ourselves. It's difficult to give ourselves the praise we deserve for the accomplishments we've achieved because society has stressed that it's not virtuous to boast or brag.

So, we wait for or hope for the external acknowledgment of others.

Sitting around with humility and grace are lovely ideas. It may grant you sainthood, but it won't help you reach those lofty goals that you have set for yourself.

List your accomplishments. Keep your list handy to remind yourself how far you've come. Treat yourself for your accomplishments!

If no one knows what you have accomplished, tell them! Put your accomplishment in a company newsletter. Post it on social media. Invite someone to celebrate with you.

Acknowledge yourself *first*—and then acknowledge others!

Friends, lovers, colleagues, employers, and employees—everyone we come into contact with—need and want recognition and acknowledgement.

To your transformation!

ACKNOWLEDGMENT #3

> *But what I thought, and what I still think, and always will, is that she saw me. Nobody else has ever seen me—me, Jenny Gluckstein—like that. Not my parents, not Julian, not even Meena. Love is one thing—recognition is something else.*
> —Peter S. Beagle, *Tamsin*

Your closest friends, the one(s) you keep in your life for the longest time are the people who recognize you for *who* you are, *warts* and all, and who love you for *who* you are!

These are, generally, the same people who *you* love, *warts* and all.

You know their strengths. You know their weaknesses. You have seen them at their worst, and you have seen them at their best.

You love them in spite of the fact that they may have accidentally hurt your feelings because they made a mistake. Apologies were made. You have forgiven them their shortcomings because they always have *your* best interest at heart.

But most importantly—they *get* you! They recognize you for who you are! Sometimes they recognize you better than you recognize yourself.

There is nothing more fulfilling than being acknowledged for who you are! Everyone wants to be seen! Recognition is the greatest sense of being present in life.

When you find those people who recognize you, keep them close, keep them long, and treasure them. Nurture their spirits in kind. Take the time to acknowledge them.

To your continued transformation!

CHAPTER 3

ADVENTURE

One way to get the most out of life is to look upon it as an adventure.

—William Feather

We wake up every day and have the opportunity to choose our attitude. We can start the day with drudgery and dismay, complaining about our lot in life, grumbling about having to go to work and not having the things that will make us joyful and happy. *Or* we can start the day with a smile on our face. We can look toward the future of the next twelve to sixteen hours with wonder and excitement. We can choose to have a sense of adventure about what may wait in the day ahead and see it all as a challenge to take on with new and fresh ideas.

Your challenge this week is to do just that. Approach each day like an adventure.

You do not have to leave the house to do it!

Life is not perfect. It's not wrapped up in a bow, neatly packaged.

Life is messy. It spills over and gets tangled up into knots.

Enjoy the journey of your life. Every step, every day is a new adventure!

Take it slow or fast. Travel at your own pace. When you stumble and fall, that's part of the adventure—relish that part too and take whatever positive things you can from that experience.

Just enjoy the trip!

Life is an adventure, it's not a package tour. (Eckhart Tolle)

To your transformation!

ADVENTURE #2

> *Whatever course you have chosen for yourself, it will not be a chore but an adventure if you bring to it a sense of the glory of striving.*
>
> —David Sarnoff

When you strive to be the best you can be at whatever you choose for yourself, your path will automatically become an adventure.

Whether that path is the road to becoming
the best employee on your career path *or*
the best at your chosen sport *or*
a world-renowned poet or chef *or*
the best parent or spouse *or*
the best teacher or friend—

whatever your goal—when you choose to excel, adventure awaits!

Adventure is automatic because, as you practice your craft, you hone your skills to make yourself a better person in this area. This practice takes you on a journey as you seek improvement. *Any* journey is an adventure!

Your adventure can be external as you go through schooling, training, or other ways of developing yourself.

Your adventure can be internal as you go through mental and/or emotional expansion—as you open your mind to new ideas and/or open your heart to people, to love, and to discovering yourself.

Your adventure is never a straight path, so don't expect it to be an easy path. It takes twists and turns much like a winding road.

There is no certainty; there is only adventure. (Roberto Assagioli)

To your transformation!

ADVENTURE #3

It is only in adventure that some people succeed in knowing themselves—in finding themselves.

—Andre Gide

Approaching life as an adventure will bring you to finding out who you are. I am sure you've heard people say, "I'm looking for myself," or, "I need to find myself." People have been using those phrases for eons, and in the journey to "find themselves," they have gone on adventures of many different types:

Adventures of intellectual pursuits
Adventures in search of spiritual enlightenment
Adventures for physical development and connection to Mother Earth
Adventure for the sake of excitement and exploration of the soul

Adventure is a daily occurrence if you make it happen. Adventure is your attitude.

Adventure is overcoming your fears and tackling your desires while maintaining your integrity.

Adventure is balance—yes, balance! That's because there is adventure in figuring out how to "have it all" with balance.

It takes finesse to figure it out and make it work. It's important to figure out what makes you happy—what you want from life.

Make lists of those things that you want and that make you happy.

List the people you want *in* your life.

Choose the work situation from which you can arrange to get and have the things you listed.

Choose the living situation/location where you can get access to the people and things that make you happy.

Include everything that you do for *fun* and adventure on your lists.

To your balance!

To your transformation!

CHAPTER 4

ANXIETY

Just because I can't explain the feelings causing my anxiety, doesn't make them less valid.

—Lauren Elizabeth

Anxiety has become the most prevalent and debilitating mental condition of the twenty-first century. It knows no age or gender barrier. Nor does it discriminate according to race, ethnicity, or religious belief. We are all subject to its widespread tendrils of manifested angst.

Not all anxiety is bad however. It lets us know when we need to spring into action. We feel anxious before a job interview, for example, which lets us know that we need to be at our best. If we play sports, we may feel anxiety before a game so that we play to our strengths. We may feel anxious when walking on a dark street alone, which lets us know to be wary of strangers or danger lurking in shadows ahead. Anxiety is meant to keep us safe and to keep us performing well.

Extreme levels of anxiety can be immobilizing, however, and that kind of anxiety can feel terrible. A person could be having an anxiety attack, and no one would even know because it happens on the inside. It feels like your brain isn't working properly because you can't process your thoughts. Sometimes it feels like your body isn't working properly either because you get knots in your stomach and other physical sensations, like

13

sweating or itching or twitches and heart palpitations. Sometimes it feels like you can't breathe.

Many times, you may not know *why* you feel anxious. You just *do*! You can't explain it. People may ask, "What's wrong?" and you can't answer, which makes you feel worse.

Your challenge this week is to just be with yourself and just be with your own level of anxiety.

Accept your anxiety as a part of you.

We all have anxiety. No one is exempt. We just have different levels of it. Recognize *your* level of anxiety.

Be gentle with yourself and know that you're doing the best that you can. At the end of the day, tell yourself gently, "I love you. You did the best you could today. And even if you didn't accomplish all you had planned, I love you!"

To your transformation!

ANXIETY #2

> Anxiety isn't something that goes away; it's something you learn to control.
>
> —unknown

There are many strategies that can be used to minimize levels of anxiety.

The first step is to be aware of your anxiety and tell yourself that it's okay to have anxiety.

The more you fight against it, the more it will fight back to keep its ground. Therefore, your anxiety will become stronger and more prevalent, rather than being acknowledged and falling into the background.

Anxiety is like a small child needing attention! If you have ever seen a small child looking for attention, notice that he or she will keep jumping up and down; doing bigger and bigger tricks, the child will continue trying to get attention from someone, anyone who will look at him or her and acknowledge his or her existence and his or her "wonderfulness." Once children get the acknowledgement they crave, they will go play with their friends or find other activities—until they pop up again needing more attention.

Anxiety is just the same. It craves attention. When you experience it, acknowledge its existence and its necessity (healthy levels of anxiety keep you safe and at your best). It will diminish some when it's acknowledged. *And* it will come and go. Just acknowledge it every time you notice it—just like a friend who comes to visit.

Exercise regularly! Moving your body is important for multiple reasons.

Physical fitness helps you to feel good about yourself and how you look. And how you feel *physically* increases your level of self-esteem, which lowers your anxiety. When you feel strong, you *are* strong, both physically and mentally. Ironic maybe, but true!

Exercise will also boost your serotonin levels, which will improve mood and brain function.

Have fun! We forget and get too busy to add *fun* into our daily lives. However, having fun is essential to releasing stress and curing anxiety.

When we were children, we had lower levels of anxiety, and we played, either alone or with friends. As adults, we forget to play. So, go out and play! Have fun!

Think back to what gave you pleasure when you were younger. What made you laugh? Go out and do those things, either alone or with friends. Plan them if you have to. Or even better, be spontaneous!

Play a game, go listen to music or play music, play a sport or watch sports, play catch, go swimming, take a dance class, take pottery lessons (playing with clay), or just buy Play-Doh. Jump rope, play hopscotch, paint, play board games, play bingo, go to a museum, or go to an amusement park.

Be creative! But *act now*!

To your transformation!

> *Nothing diminishes anxiety faster than action.*
> —Walter Anderson

ANXIETY #3

*Worry pretends to be necessary, but serves no useful purpose.
If you want to conquer the anxiety of life, live in the moment,
live in the breath.*

—Eckhart Tolle

Worry causes stress, frown lines, wrinkles, and negative emotions.

Worry is about the future, about things that may never happen. It's especially useless to worry over things you have no control over.

I remember when my eldest sister was diagnosed with cancer. My other sister asked me, "What's wrong with you? You act like nothing is wrong. You act like you are happy and carefree when you should be worried."

Now those may not have been her exact words, but her words were similar.

My response was simple. "I know that my sister is ill. Worrying about it isn't going to change the situation. Worrying isn't going to make her well or help her or me in any way. Being optimistic, on the other hand, just might help make both of us feel better!"

When you change the way you look at things, the things
you look at change. (Wayne Dyer)

We have lots of life to live in the present moment. Get up, go out, and live it. Let whatever you do today be enough! Stop worrying.

To your transformation!

CHAPTER 5

BLESSINGS

> *Life is not always easy to live, but the opportunity to do so is a blessing beyond comprehension. In the process of living, we will face struggles, many of which will cause us to suffer and to experience pain.*
>
> —L. Lionel Kenrick

Many things come to us during our lifetimes. Events occur that cause happiness, and we celebrate with family and friends.

Other things happen that cause devastating consequences, and we experience pain and sadness beyond anything that we think we can endure.

We have the blessings of strength to find our way through the muck and the mire of devastating ordeals. Whether your experience is the loss of a loved one, divorce, or illness, grief, loneliness, and despair can seem endless.

Somehow, with the grace of God and with the help of friends and family, we survive!

We are blessed to have other people in our lives to offer support in our times of need.

We have the blessing of strength to help us with the conflicts in our lives.

Arguments with our loved ones, which cause stress and discomfort, are aided by the blessing of insight and the blessing of love.

We have the blessing of intelligence to solve problems that may interfere with our goals.

Your challenge is to count your blessings starting this week. Blessings are everywhere, even where you don't expect them!

Look and you will see them.

> You never know where a blessing can come from. (Teena Marie)

To your transformation!

BLESSINGS #2

> *Some people come into our life as a blessing, while others come into our life as a lesson, so love them for who they are instead of judging them for who they are not.*
>
> —Yolanda Hadid

Look for the blessing in all people! While there are lessons to be learned, you are blessed through the learning.

After all, you or I would not want to remain stagnant on one intellectual or emotional level for all of eternity, would we? I wouldn't.

Well, it is *my* mission to learn from others continuously.

Life is a journey, *so* to learn from everyone and everything that we come into contact with on this journey is what makes things interesting and keeps me young.

I have been blessed by *all* of the people who have crossed into my life so far because I have learned something from all of them.

All of the people who are in my life on a regular basis teach me love, tolerance, compassion, openness, kindness, and skills too numerous to list here.

I am grateful every day for all of them and for their presence in my life.

The people who are no longer in my life have taught me insight and forgiveness. This includes how to forgive myself and others too.

Forgiveness isn't just a blessing you deliver to another human being Forgiveness is also a gift you give yourself. (Robin S. Sharma)

Being grateful and counting your blessings every day is a blessing in itself!

Imagine this: Everything you hold dear is taken away from you—your family, job, business, home, everything. It's all gone!

What do you do? You realize that what you already have is so much more important than what you don't have. You realize how blessed, how successful, and how happy you already are.

Now, in your reality, can see that? It's like that movie *It's a Wonderful Life*, when George finds out what the world would look like if he had never existed and realizes that his life is blessed with friends and family and filled with love, even though times seem bleak and filled with despair.

Maybe you could be happier, but if you think about it, your life may already be pretty great.

Every night when you turn off your bedroom light, take a second to count your blessings. Think of three things for which you are grateful. Write those three things down on a piece of paper. Keep this list next to your bed. And each night, add another three things. They can be simple things. I am grateful for my cozy bed or for my warm socks or for the roof over my head or for the fact that I made it through the day in one piece. Watch your list grow longer and longer, day by day.

Do that, and you won't have to worry about whether or not you're happy—because you will know that you have been blessed!

Every day I feel is a blessing from God. And I consider it a new beginning. Yeah, everything is beautiful. (Prince)

To your transformation!

BLESSINGS #3

There is inestimable blessing in a cheerful spirit. When the soul throws its windows wide open, letting in the sunshine, and presenting to all who see it the evidence of its gladness, it is not only happy, but it has an unspeakable power of doing good.

—Orison Swett Marden

So accordingly, *be happy* to spread happy!

When you are happy and act happy, you will spread goodness! You will have the natural tendency to perform acts of kindness.

I am sure that you've heard the phrase "fake it until you make it."

That applies here very well. If you aren't feeling happy, fake it!

Act happy, and you will be happy.

What do happy people do? They smile a lot! They talk to other people. They help others. They are kind and caring and giving of themselves.

Acting "as if" you're happy doesn't mean you have to be phony or inauthentic. Instead, it's about bringing out the best in yourself.

As long as your motivation is in the right place, faking it until you make it can be an effective way to make your goals become reality. Just make sure you're interested in changing yourself on the inside, not simply trying to change other people's perceptions of you.

When you focus on being a blessing, God makes sure that you are always blessed in abundance. (Joel Osteen)

To your transformation!

CHAPTER 6

BREATHE

> *Let go of the battle. Breathe quietly and let it be. Let your body relax and your heart soften. Open to whatever you experience without fighting.*
> —Jack Kornfield, *A Path with Heart: A Guide through the Perils and Promises of Spiritual Life*

The holiday time of year is one of the most stressful times for millions of people, both young and old. While the holiday season may bring joy, it also brings many pressures. For many, there is the pressure to be perfect:

- To perform well in school (midyear exams)
- To finish the year on a good note on the job

Financial stress has pressure as well:

- To buy gifts and pay monthly bills
- To find the "right" gift

Other stressors and pressures include:

- Pressure on relationships (spending time with family/friends)
- Not enough time to "get it all done"

- Loneliness
- Loss

No matter what your stressor or anxiety—remember to *breathe*. Breathing reduces stress.

Your challenge this week is to practice breathing.

Inhale—exhale—inhale—exhale. Repeat.

To your transformation!

BREATHE #2

> *When life is foggy, path is unclear and mind is dull, remember your breath. It has the power to give you the peace. It has the power to resolve the unsolved equations of life.*
>
> —Amit Ray

When you are feeling stressed, like there is nowhere to run and no way to solve your problems:

- Take one long, slow, deep breath. (Try counting to eight or ten as you inhale slowly.)
- Exhale—slowly counting to ten or fifteen while you breathe out.
- Repeat this process *ten* times.

When you are finished, call a friend or family member or teacher or a hotline—anyone! —so that you can debrief your stress.

If you don't want to talk, take a bath, go for a walk/run, listen to soothing music, or visit a pet store and play with the animals.

Practice stress reduction techniques!

Meditation, yoga, tai chi, massage, visualization, mindful exercise, rhythmic movement, self-hypnosis, and self-relaxation techniques are some things you can use to help reduce stress.

To your transformation!

BREATHE #3

Breathe in deeply to bring your mind home to your body. Then look at, or think of, the person triggering this emotion: With mindfulness, you can see that she is unhappy, that she is suffering. You can see her wrong perceptions. You can see that she is not beautiful when she says things that are unkind.
—Thich Nhat Hanh

Sometimes a person, people, or external events trigger our stress.

With mindfulness, we can recognize that person or those people for where they are and not take their words or action personally.

With mindfulness, we can see that events are just the way things happen and not our fault.

We can have acceptance of people and events and take action to make our lives change for the better.

When we breathe and are aware of our breath, we create our mindfulness of self, therefore developing mindfulness of our surroundings (others/events).

With your breath, you can create power over your own life.

To your transformation!

CHAPTER 7

CHANGING

Life is 10 percent what you experience and 90 percent how you respond to it.

—Dorothy M. Neddermeyer

We spend all of our lives responding to the things that happen due to the fact that life is a series of reactions.Ralph Waldo Emerson said the law of cause and effect is the "law of laws."

The most important lesson involving human conduct and interaction is seen in the cosmic law of cause and effect: "For every action there is an equal and opposite reaction."

Sometimes we think that we have to respond to certain actions or events a specific way. We think that our behavior, thoughts, and feelings are predetermined by what happens. However, the exact opposite is true!

We have a choice as to how we will respond or react to the things that happen around us and to us. We freely choose our thoughts, feelings, and actions every moment of every day. If we are not happy with our reactions, we are free to change them.

Your challenge this week is to consider changing one of your reactions to things that do not make you happy. For example, perhaps you get impatient while waiting in line at the store (impatience is a chosen reaction to waiting). Or perhaps you get angry while driving (anger is a chosen reaction to traffic or other driving situations). Both of these are examples only!

Think for yourself, of a reaction that *you* have that you would like to change and work to change it—for your happiness!

To your transformation!

> *If you don't like something, change it; if you can't change it, change the way you think about it.*
> —Mary Engelbreit

CHANGING #2

> *Don't settle: Don't finish crappy books. If you don't like the menu, leave the restaurant. If you're not on the right path, get off it.*
> —Chris Brogan

Change is a very frightening and scary thing.

People stay in the same boring or meaningless job that they hate because they are afraid to make a change.

Couples stay in hurtful relationships because one or both of them are scared of change.

Sometimes a person will live in the city that he or she grew up in for his or her entire life, not because he or she loves living there but because it is too intimidating to move.

Change can be terrifying!

It takes courage to admit that you want something different.

Yet admitting your desire is the first and most necessary step for change to occur.

> Your vision will become clear only when you look into your heart. Who looks outside, dreams. Who looks inside, awakens. (Carl Jung)

To your transformation!

CHANGING #3

> *You can't always control what goes on outside. But you can always control what goes on inside.*
>
> —Wayne Dyer

I used to fight with myself and try to push away any emotions that I didn't want to have.

These solitary shadow fights caused quite the hype and would last for hours as I went around and around with myself.

If I was sad about something, I would try to push it down or push it away. I had silent conversations with myself disallowing this emotion. I viewed "sad" as negative, and I didn't want it to be in my personal space.

This practice caused "sad" to stay for long periods of time, digging in its heels and making a home in my brain and in my heart.

My *change* is to accept whatever feeling I now have and view it as a temporary guest—without labeling it as negative or positive. It's just a feeling. Some examples are sad, lonely, or angry.

I sit quietly and experience the feeling and say to it, "You are welcome in my personal space."

I also remind myself that I am love. I am courage. I am strength.

> Believe in yourself and all that you are. Know that there is something inside of you that is greater than any obstacle. (Christian D. Larson)

Whatever feeling is visiting that day stays for shorter moments now.

To your continued transformation!

> *Peace is the result of retraining your mind to process life as it is, rather than as you think it should be.*
>
> —Wayne W. Dyer

CHAPTER 8

CHARACTER

Character is what you know you are, not what others think you have.

—Marva Collins

Your *character* represents your mental and moral disposition. It is the essence of your being, the very nature of who you are, defining you as a person.

Some people put a person's character in one of two categories—good or bad. Often, however, it isn't that simple.

According to standards of society, actions can be categorized as good (acceptable) or bad (unacceptable). Actions do not always define character.

So, I propose two situations to ponder:

1. A wealthy person may give an abundance of money to the less fortunate for his or her own gratification and self-serving purposes. Is he or she of good character because he or she gives to the less fortunate?
2. A young teen may go into a store and steal food for the dinner table because his or her parent is working two jobs and struggles to feed the family. The teen has the character to take care of his or her family, however, has not been given the skills to work within the

societal framework to make it happen in an acceptable fashion. Is this teen of good character?

Other people will be quick to judge you by what you do. They think they know who you are by what they see or what they think they see. You alone know the reasons for your actions. You alone know the makeup of your character.

Your challenge this week is to examine the content of your character. Is your character all *you* want it to be? Are you living up to your own standards?

Rise to be the *best* you can be!

To your transformation!

CHARACTER #2

> *It was* character *that got us out of bed, commitment that moved us into action, and discipline that enabled us to follow through.*
>
> —Zig Ziglar

So, if you're reading this, you're out of bed and into the action of starting your day! And some days, just the action of getting started is hard.

Some days it feels like a thousand weights are holding you down, and you don't want to move. You're tired and lack the energy to get going.

You hear the little voice inside your head telling you, *No!* It's saying, *I don't want to* or *I can't.*

Being in action and staying in action comes down to building and developing solid character.

Solid character starts with *integrity*, which means doing what you said you would do when you said you would do it. It means doing a great job at everything you do; going above and beyond the ordinary; and showing up and doing it, even when nobody is watching you.

Integrity includes being *honest*—pure and simple—no beating about the bush, no lies, no omissions, and no avoiding the unpleasant. Be forward and honest. Be in communication.

Be *giving* of *yourself.* If you have to be the one to show up or to stay late, then you are the one. Do what it takes to get it done. *And* do an excellent job!

Be *accountable.* Take responsibility for yourself and your actions. Own it!

Have *self-control.* Be a good example for others. Be a good role model. No one likes someone who seems out of control or who makes bad decisions. Someone who exhibits self-control makes good decisions. In other words, you don't drink and drive, you are wise with dating, you manage your social life, and you do your work and responsibilities with integrity.

> Our character is basically a composite of our habits. Because they are consistent, often unconscious patterns, they constantly, daily, express our character. (Stephen Covey)

To your transformation!

CHARACTER #3

> *Goodness is about* character—*integrity, honesty, kindness, generosity, moral courage, and the like. More than anything else, it is about how we treat other people.*
> —Dennis Prager

It is not our position in life to sit in judgment of others and determine if they are "good" or "bad."

Someone with good character doesn't sit in judgment of others and decide whether or not other people have good character (unless they are assigned to do so in a court of law or other judicial office, in which case a person is assigned to judge the actions of another).

Part of being of "good" character is to be judgment free and to allow others to be themselves without worry.

However, it is not our concern what others think of us or what they may believe. It is up to us to be true to ourselves and true to our character. We must own our behavior and be responsible for our actions. We must own our own standards of excellence of character and reach to achieve those standards.

One of the best ways to improve your character is to reach out and help others. In small ways every day, improve someone's day with a smile or by lending a hand. Be creative with your gestures of kindness.

When our purpose is true and our agenda clearly in pursuit of helping others, the first gain is that others receive what they need. *And* as a secondary gain, our hearts fill with love, and our lives fill with joy as we recognize that we have brought ease or happiness into another person's life.

Continue to examine your actions every day and change yourself as you need to in order to reach your goals and to meet your high standards of character.

> A good character is the best tombstone. Those who loved you and were helped by you will remember you when forget-me-nots have withered. Carve your name on hearts, not on marble. (Charles Spurgeon)

To your transformation!

CHAPTER 9

CHOICE

CHOICE #1

Attitude is a choice. Happiness is a choice. Optimism is a choice. Kindness is a choice. Giving is a choice. Respect is a choice. Whatever choice you make makes you. Choose wisely.
> —Roy T. Bennett, *The Light in the Heart*

We all are the sum of all of the choices we make throughout our lives, good or bad, right or wrong, big and small.

We make choices everyday about everything. Our choices are based on our beliefs and values.

> Beliefs are choices. First you choose your beliefs. Then your beliefs affect your choices. (Roy T. Bennett)

Then we surround ourselves with the things and people who follow the same or similar choices or set of values and beliefs.

We make choices based on what we like and don't like and on what we want and do not want in our lives.

Our choices lead us down paths that we like and some that we don't like. We then have the ability to make changes to reevaluate the choices we've made.

If we don't like what has happened in our lives or what is happening now, we can make different choices. We can change the path of our lives.

It's scary to make changes, but it can also be exciting!

Your challenge this week is to look at your choices. Evaluate where your choices are leading you and look to see if you want to make different choices.

Ask yourself, do I want a new path?

A new or different relationship?

A new or different career?

A new or different living arrangement?

A new or different approach to your health/well-being?

A new or different car, wardrobe, friend—anything that might need a change?

> Until a person can say deeply and honestly, "I am what I am today because of the choices I made yesterday," that person cannot say, "I choose otherwise. (Stephen R. Covey, *The 7 Habits of Highly Effective People: Powerful Lessons in Personal Change*)

Do not let fear stop you from making a different choice.

You are waiting to blossom! *To your transformation!*

CHOICE #2

> *You are not the victim of the world, but rather the master of your own destiny. It is your choices and decisions that determine your destiny.*
>
> —Roy T. Bennett

So many people, myself included, get stuck in "victim mode," thinking we are victims of our circumstances.

We think, *If only that didn't happen, then my life would have been better or happier.* Or we tell ourselves, *If they had treated me differently, I would have been different—richer, better, thinner.*

We create blame for our situation—instead of looking at the choices that we have made.

Now you know you don't choose everything that happens in life.

Ultimately, we may not have chosen to be abused as a child, for example, but we may have chosen to feel angry and unforgiving about it. That attitude creates your future. Your choices about circumstances create your life.

You may have been born into poverty. If you choose to remain in poverty and feel sorry for your circumstances, then that is how you will live forevermore. If you choose wealth and abundance, then you will work hard and change your conditions.

Life is a choice! Whether we make our choices consciously or subconsciously through active decision or by indecision and allowing things to happen, we are making choices *all* of the time.

To your transformation!

> *You cannot control what happens to you, but you can control the way you think about all the events. You always have a choice. You can choose to face them with a positive mental attitude.*
> —Roy T. Bennett, *The Light in the Heart*

CHOICE #3

> *I can do anything I want.*
> *Be with anyone I want.*
> *And it'll be my choice.*
> —Tahereh Mafi, *Ignite Me*

The ultimate problem with the freedom to choose is that many people get confused by too much choice. This is especially true in a monogamous relationship.

Many people, regardless of age, get distracted from their primary relationships by beauty and sexual attraction.

Females and males alike look at other healthy, attractive men and women with desire. This tendency to "look" at the physical beauty of other people of the opposite sex, or the same sex if you are of such persuasion, is totally natural. It would be unnatural or unhealthy not to appreciate the beauty of other human beings.

We all want to be appreciated for our sexuality and want others to appreciate their own. It's the natural order of life. It's primal, yes, but natural too.

The difference is, as human people with intelligence, we can choose not to always *act* on our primal thoughts and feelings. We can choose instead to *act* on our promises to stay true to one mate in a marriage or in a committed relationship.

> I fell in love with him. But I don't just stay with him by default as if there's no one else available to me. I stay with him because I choose to, every day that I wake up, every day that we fight or lie to each other or disappoint each other. I choose him over and over again, and he chooses me. (Veronica Roth, *Allegiant*)

If you do not choose your significant other every day, perhaps it's time to take a look at your relationship and think about making a change. Maybe something is missing. Maybe you need to open your lines of communication and reset your expectations.

Then see what happens!

To your transformation!

> *Maturity is when you stop complaining and making excuses, and start making changes.*
> —Roy T. Bennett, *The Light in the Heart*

CHAPTER 10

COMFORT ZONE

You never change your life *until you step out of your comfort zone; change begins at the end of your comfort zone.*
—Roy T. Bennett

If we are lucky, and I believe that life is filled with luck—some are luckier than others—we start our lives with people who push us to be our best.

In a perfect world, parents want their children to be the best they can be and to reach their fullest potential. They do what they can to push their children to reach their lofty goals. Effective parents teach their children that they can be successful outside the parameters of their comfort zone.

In school, you have teachers who push you to reach your best. When you are not achieving, your teachers push you to do more; to work harder; to give it your "best effort"; and to strive to be better or go beyond the limits of your "comfortable" behavior academically, civically, or socially. Good teachers promote leadership!

If you are lucky enough to go to college, you are encouraged to apply to schools that are considered "reach" schools. These are colleges and universities that may be too good for you—schools that may or may not accept you as a candidate, schools that are outside your scholarly ability and outside your comfort zone. If you are accepted, you are amazed, excited, scared, and raised to a new level of awe at your accomplishment.

Uncomfortable? Yes, but also in a position of ability for new achievements.

> Comfort is your biggest trap and coming out of comfort zone your biggest challenge. (Manoj Arora)

Your challenge this week is to choose one area to step out of your comfort zone and make a change in your life.

To your transformation!

COMFORT ZONE #2

> *We are so accustomed to the comforts of "I cannot", "I do not want to" and "it is too difficult" that we forget to realize when we stop doing things for ourselves and expect others to dance around us, we are not achieving greatness. We have made ourselves weak.*
>
> —Pandora Poikilos, *Excuse Me, My Brains Have Stepped Out*

I hear the following words too often, either from my friends, people I work with, family members, or others: "I can't." "I don't want to." "It's so hard."

I am guilty of feeling these same sentiments, of saying these same thoughts in my head.

I feel frustrated and sad because I know that there is so much more in life. Greatness in life lies in wait just outside the boundary of our "comfort zone".

Yet no one ever said it was going to be easy. The first step can be very challenging. Sometimes we need someone to push us when we have difficulty pushing ourselves.

We can start with small changes in our boundaries—stepping outside of our comfort zone little by little. You don't have to start by jumping out of airplanes or bungee jumping from the Golden Gate Bridge, which is illegal, so don't do that! Start small.

If the TV is on all evening, turn it off and try reading the newspaper or reading a book instead. Better yet, join a book club and go out one evening a month to a book club meeting.

If you are sedentary, try an exercise video or take an exercise class. Start with a YouTube video to see what you like before you join.

If you want to travel, take a weekend trip to a nearby tourist attraction that you have never seen.

If you want to improve your dating circle, join an online dating site. (you don't have to date but joining is the first step!)

You get the idea. Be creative. Make new possibilities! Sure, you might have a little anxiety. *But* take a breath, count to ten, breathe.

Have *fun* stepping out of your comfort zone!

To your transformation!

> *Sometimes we have to step out of our comfort zones. We have to break the rules. And we have to discover the sensuality of fear. We need to face it, challenge it, dance with it.*
> —Kyra Davis

COMFORT ZONE #3

> *Coming out of your comfort zone is tough in the beginning, chaotic in the middle, and awesome in the end ... because in the end, it shows you a whole new world!!*
> *Make an attempt.*
> —Manoj Arora, *From the Rat Race to Financial Freedom*

In all areas of your life, stepping out of your comfort zone may transform your world.

When you are in a relationship with another person, it's important to "stretch" outside of the parameters of your comfort in order to accommodate the other person's needs and requests. You often have to give up something of yourself, whether it is time or energy to devote yourself to the needs of your significant other. However, the benefits that you reap generally outweigh the cost.

Your relationship becomes closer. You develop trust and a higher level of intimacy.

At your place of work, leaders are born out of pushing past and through levels of discomfort. Bosses may push employees harder than they would push themselves, leading to promotions or higher levels of pay. Employees who push past company goals often move up within the company or seek positions elsewhere. Those employees then go on to roles more suited to their leadership behaviors.

> Step out of your comfort zone. Comfort zones, where your unrealized dreams are buried, are the enemies of achievement. Leadership begins when you step outside your comfort zone. (Roy T. Bennett)

Some of the benefits of stretching your comfort zone include but are not limited to improving your brain activity, increasing resilience, expanding self-confidence, and being challenged to improve yourself. And it may even help prevent depression.

To your transformation!

CHAPTER 11

COMMITMENT

COMMITMENT #1

There is no love or relationship without Commitment.
Unless commitment is made, there are only promises and
hopes ... but no plans. —Peter Drucker

We, as a society or group, seem to be afraid of commitment.

But what is commitment? And why are people afraid of it?

By definition, commitment means, "a promise to do something." Whether it is a promise to do something for ourselves, someone else or for a group or community, it remains the same obligation or premise of having to do something.

Some people are afraid of the work involved in completing the promise or the task of the commitment.

We, all of us, get stuck in our own thoughts of self-doubt and self-talk. We tell ourselves that we can't possibly do it (whatever "it" is, in the realm of commitment)

We think to ourselves that maybe we should *run away*!

Maybe we should *quit now*!

We doubt our ability to succeed and, therefore, hesitate to make the commitment in the first place.

You always have two choices: your commitment versus your fear. (Sammy Davis, Jr.)

Your challenge this week is to make one *commitment*, however small, that you can keep—whether it is being on time for a class, calling someone, setting a date, finishing a task, starting a task, sending an email. You get the idea. Then celebrate your success and share your accomplishment with someone!

To your transformation!

COMMITMENT #2

The quality of a person's life is in direct proportion to their commitment to excellence, regardless of their chosen field of endeavor.

—Vince Lombardi

Many people believe that, in order to make a commitment, you have to give up a part of yourself or your freedom. They do not realize that, while meeting the promise of the commitment, they actually gain so many things.

When you keep a commitment to yourself or others, you might notice that you feel good about yourself. For example, if you want to lose weight and you successfully passed up dessert because you stood by your commitment to eat healthy, you might have smiled to yourself for your success. Or when you took your car to be serviced, even though you would rather have been out with your friends after work, but you kept your commitment to take care of your vehicle, you may have felt satisfied with yourself for following through on your commitment with your responsibility.

You gain a sense of self-satisfaction, self-fulfillment, and integrity for following through on your commitments.

Think about the person you want to be. Think about the person you are now. Do those two people match? Can the person you are now be bigger? Better? Larger? More honest, more giving? If the answer is *yes*, then start by keeping commitments, however small.

> You will be able to build yourself *up, up, up*!
> There's no abiding success without commitment. (Tony Robbins)

To your transformation!

COMMITMENT #3

> *Passion is the quickest to develop, and the quickest to fade. Intimacy develops more slowly, and commitment more gradually still.*
>
> —Robert Sternberg

When we hear the word *commitment*, many people automatically think about personal relationships or love relationships. We often hear about "lack of commitment" or "commitment phobic" men or women.

It seems that young people are all on a mission to meet "the perfect partner." (Did I just make up the name of next great dating site?) Yet, no one is in a hurry to make the step toward a lasting commitment. Nor should they be!

Commitment is not something to be rushed into haphazardly without thought or vision, like "jump first and ask questions later."

No.

However, sometimes commitments go unspoken and last for years. In many cases, love relationships develop into something more when couples decide to live together. Two people make the commitment to have a lasting relationship. Further traditional commitments sometimes aren't necessary.

> Mature love is composed and sustaining; a celebration of commitment, companionship, and trust. (H. Jackson Brown, Jr.)

Some people recognize the development of themselves through their own commitments and the development of their relationships over time. Some people are happy with the status quo. Both groups of people are right, because that is what makes them satisfied and content.

For myself, I know the following to be true:

> The relationship between commitment and doubt is by no means an antagonistic one. Commitment is healthiest when it's not without doubt but in spite of doubt. (Rollo May)

When I *want* something, I always have fear. I am afraid to make that final commitment. I doubt that I can *do it*. After all, it might not be "right"! But I make the commitment, and then—I fight for it!

I might stumble along the way. After all, I am human. I work hard, and I make mistakes. But I have some *great* results!

To your *great* results! To *your* commitments!

And *to your transformation!*

CHAPTER 12

COMPASSION

COMPASSION #1

If you want others to be happy, practice compassion. If you want to be happy, practice compassion.
—Dalai Lama XIV, *The Art of Happiness*

Compassion is closely related to empathy though not quite the same thing. Compassion is the feeling you have to be *motivated to act* to relieve the suffering of others.

Those who are suffering can be other people or other living creatures. Your acts to alleviate their suffering can be on a grand scale, or they can be small, simple acts that help the sufferer in a minimal way.

Your simple desire to help is the beginning of compassionate thought, but true compassion is defined as an act.

So, your challenge this week is to notice your acts of compassion. How do you help others? How do you help yourself?

If your compassion does not include yourself, it is incomplete. (Jack Kornfield, *Buddha's Little Instruction Book*)

To your transformation!

43

COMPASSION #2

"Self-absorption in all its forms kills empathy, let alone compassion. When we focus on ourselves, our world contracts as our problems and preoccupations loom large. But when we focus on others, our world expands. Our own problems drift to the periphery of the mind and so seem smaller, and we increase our capacity for connection—or compassionate action.

—Daniel Goleman, *Social Intelligence: The New Science of Human Relationships*

Many people believe that compassion is innate, and you either have it or you don't. But studies have been done that prove that compassion can be taught, and the brain can be reframed to build compassion.

Both adults and children can learn to be compassionate through the use of meditation and the practice of compassionate acts.

One simple way to show compassion would be to smile at strangers and at your loved ones. You never know how a smile might brighten someone's day. Open the door for the person behind you or in front of you, especially if the other person has his or her hands full with packages or is busy with toddlers. Say encouraging words to others. You never know what a difference a few kind words might make in someone's day.

Motivate another, either by your example or by your words. Be a role model to a younger person. Share a hug, a handshake, or a pat on the back with someone who looks like he or she could use some encouragement. Or even if the person doesn't look like they need encouragement, give it anyway! It's free!

Use politeness often. Please and thank you go a long way. Compliment the people in your life, the ones you see every day but generally overlook, like the train conductor, the pharmacist, the grocer, or the barista.

Practice acts of kindness daily!

Help someone with his or her to-do list!

Spend time nurturing relationships with family and friends. A phone call goes a long way.

To your transformation!

COMPASSION #3

Compassion asks us to go where it hurts, to enter into the places of pain, to share in brokenness, fear, confusion, and anguish. Compassion challenges us to cry out with those in misery, to mourn with those who are lonely, to weep with those in tears. Compassion requires us to be weak with the weak, vulnerable with the vulnerable, and powerless with the powerless. Compassion means full immersion in the condition of being human.

—Henri J. M. Nouwen

Compassion asks that we walk in the shoes of another.

It's fully immersing ourselves in another person and understanding what it's like to be him or her and what it's like to live his or her life and then acting to alleviate his or her suffering.

Compassion carries with it no prejudice and no judgment—simply love carried out with good will.

Ask yourself, Will I judge this man or woman for being in this predicament? Or in this pain?

Or will I simply help him or her?

Love and goodwill start at home.

Love yourself.

Have compassion for yourself without judgment.

Take care of yourself, and then take care of others.

Do both judgment free!

To your transformation!

CHAPTER 13

COMPATIBILITY

Support, motivation, and help—those are the three things you need as "partners" to keep sustaining your 'compatible" relationship.

—Ifeoluwa Egbetade

Compatibility equals the ability to work with little to no conflict and have "mutual" interest and desire to achieve the same goals.

Therefore, compatibility is *not* a characteristic that is found only in romantic partnerships but in all arenas of life.

To achieve your most harmonious lifestyle, match your values with your career partnerships, your friendships, and your romantic relationship and then you will find compatibility.

Your challenge this week is to identify the compatible areas of your life.

Where do you find support?

Where do you find motivation?

Is your career providing the motivation that you need? Do administrators provide support and help? Are colleagues compatible?

Look at your long-term friendships and identify the common goals/ values that you share. What makes these friendships last? Do your friends provide support? Motivation?

Romantic relationships are on the friendship list! If yours is not, I challenge you to reevaluate.

To your transformation!

COMPATIBILITY #2

> *I used to think that finding the right one was about the man having a list of certain qualities. If he has them, we'd be compatible and happy. Sort of a checkmark system that was a complete failure. But I found out that a healthy relationship isn't so much about a sense of humor or intelligence or (being) attractive. It's about avoiding partners with harmful traits and personality types. And then it's about being with a good person. A good person on his own, and a good person with you. Where the space between you feels uncomplicated and happy. A good relationship is where things just work. They work because, whatever the list of qualities, whatever the reason, you happen to be really, really good together.*
> —Deb Caletti, *The Secret Life of Prince Charming*

So, you're out there in the "big game of life" looking for a significant other, and like most people, you have a list of qualities that you think are important.

The list goes something like this—good looking, thin, in shape, funny, has a job, doesn't play games, and so on.

Actually, most people ask these three questions first: Where did you grow up? Where did you go to school? What do you do for a living? Then they base their sense of compatibility on the answers to those three questions.

In real life, however, compatibility has more to do with your intellect, how you deal with conflict, how you solve problems, and how you communicate.

You have to *like* who the other person *is* on their own and who the other person is when they are with you. You have to understand what makes that person *tick*—what motivates that person.

In turn, the other person must understand what motivates and inspires you. Both of you then support and encourage one another to move toward your individual goals. And you work together toward your common goals.

This is compatibility.

It has less to do with what you do for a living or what you like to do on the weekends. If you both like to travel or you both like to hike or you both like dogs or you both like sushi or you both like to surf—whatever you like in common—well, that's just a bonus!

To your transformation!

> *Compatibility is an achievement of love; it shouldn't be its precondition.*
>
> —Alain de Botton

COMPATIBILITY #3

> *For the longest time I couldn't understand the meaning of the cliché" being* compatible"—*whether about a lover, colleague, team mate or friend. I now get it. There is so much more behind this superficial nauseatingly-pragmatic diplomatic phrase—it goes deep down to the true essence of someone, how they see the world, how they see and position themselves, how prepared/capable they are to back you,* whether they can understand who you are *and if they are prepared to break walls for you. Anything else is details.*
>
> —Iveta Cherneva

Part of "being compatible" is "building compatibility" through communication.

Compatibility may not always just happen. You have to build it!

When I am sad and I need a hug, my significant other knows that it helps to reach out and hug me. He also knows when to make a joke and turn my frown into laughter to make me feel better.

But it wasn't always so easy! I had to teach him what I needed and wanted. I had to tell him that I needed a hug in the beginning of our relationship. He had to learn that levity made some situations easier for me to handle. Time and honest communication developed our deeper compatibility.

With friends, family, or colleagues, the same is true. When they respond in an unfavorable way, communication is the only way to improve future compatibility.

Communicate simply what's true for you. Say, for example, "Your response did not help me in that situation. For support or motivation, I really needed _____."

If a friend or coworker cannot meet your request for support, then you might need to reevaluate that relationship.

To your continued transformation!

> *The length, the depth and the strength of your relationship is determined more by your compatibility in the difficult times than by your compatibility in the better times.*
>
> —Hrishikesh Agnihotri

CHAPTER 14

COMPLETENESS

What if you never meet the other half of your soul?
What if you're complete *on your own?"*

—Crestless Wave

We get inundated by media, posts in magazines, and messages in movies and on TV that imply that "we" *must* be with another person in order to be complete—that we aren't enough alone.

Choosing to be with another person is just that—a *choice*.

Each of us is *enough* alone.

When you are *complete* with yourself and love yourself, your love will emanate and spread to others, who in turn, will want to be connected to you.

Your challenge this week is to look to see if you feel complete on your own. Ask yourself the following questions:

- What if there is nothing about me that I need to fix or change? Say, "I am perfect just the way I am!"
- What makes me happy?
- What if I already have everything, I need right here inside of me?
- What if I don't have to have it all figured out?! Say, "My life is perfect!"

50

- What if everything that is happening right now is exactly what I need to grow and become the best person I can be?
  Say, "Life is perfect!"

Whether or not you are in a relationship, you cannot fully give yourself to another unless you are fully yourself first.

Give yourself the room and time you need to be complete.

> Those who travel outward seek completeness in things; those who gaze inward find sufficiency in themselves.
> (Liezi, *The Book of Master Lie*)

To your transformation!

COMPLETENESS #2

> *Being alone is not synonymous with incompleteness.*
> *Having a partner is not a precondition for* completeness.
> —Khang Kijarro Nguyen

If you want to be with another person, then look for someone else who is complete with him or herself and who complements your completeness.

Your two wholes will come together and create an awesome new being. As your similarities and differences generate new and exciting energy, you blend together and encourage one another to live life as your best selves.

Over the years, I will say that I have had the experience of being in many different relationships. And none worked until I was able to say that I am happy as myself. I am happy with my life. I can be alone if I choose. I was never fully in love with myself or fully complete before that. Therefore, my relationships had differing forms of dependence, need, blame, and resentment, which led to dissolution of love.

When you look to another person to complete you or to complete some aspect of your life or happiness, you will be left with disappointment, resentment, and blame. You end up blaming the other person for the things that you don't do in your own life and for the happiness that you cannot create for yourself.

When you are truly complete and fully in love with yourself, then you are able to love another person unconditionally as well.

True love is total acceptance of yourself *and* of the person with whom you are in a relationship.

To your transformation!

COMPLETENESS #3

> *Live a life that you do not need to take a vacation from. Live in a way that makes yearly resolutions unnecessary. Make the kind of choices that leave you Happy and Healthy ... where all of your needs are satisfied. Live a life where your only "wants" are for others to feel as good as you do.*
>
> —Gary Hopkins

How to make yourself and your life *complete* is easy. It comes down to two simple principles:

1. *Act now.*
   Don't put anything off.

   Most of us live our lives in "someday mode." Someday I will fix the hole in the wall. Someday I will talk to the cute girl/ guy in the apartment down the hall. Someday I will visit Lake Mead. Someday I will call Uncle Joe. Someday I will learn to paint, sew, swim. Someday I will call my friend and apologize for _____.

   Someday may never come.

   Whatever is on your list of things that you might want to do someday—*do it now!*

   Be happy now! Create your bliss today.

2. *Share* your *love* with others. Smile, it's contagious!

   Greet other people with joy. Give compliments freely. You have no idea how one small compliment might just make someone's day, month, or year.

Teach others—any skill or thing that you know that others ask about.

Act and share—two simple steps.

To your transformation!

CHAPTER 15

CONFIDENCE

CONFIDENCE #1

Confidence! What is it? How do we get it and how do we keep it?

Is it a coincidence that, in order to have confidence, you need to think positive?

I think not! Thinking positive leads to more positive behavior.

Confident people spend more time in positive action than in thinking.

Think of successful famous people who speak about positive things— Michael Strahan, Ryan Seacrest, and Oprah Winfrey are a few that come to mind. They think positive. But more importantly, they take action.

Point proven!

It's important to dress the part of a confident person. When was the last time that you saw someone who looked confident? Think about it for a minute. What did the person look like? What was he or she wearing? How was his or her hair combed? It's important to be well groomed and well dressed! Your outfit and hairstyle help make you feel good about yourself. (Think about that the next time you're feeling down in the dumps and stay home on the couch wearing crumpled-up pajamas—ugh!)

Exercise! The more active you are, the better you will feel about yourself, physically and emotionally. Physical activity releases endorphins, which are scientifically proven to help you feel good. This will boost your confidence. Also, better muscle tone will help you to stand taller, which will make you feel more confident.

Be kind and generous! We've been talking about helping others right along. Volunteer! When you take the emphasis off of yourself and place focus on helping others, you will feel better about yourself—instant confidence.

Give thanks for all you are and for all you have already achieved! A grateful heart is a reminder of our beginnings. It's good to remain humble and grateful for what we have.

Your challenge is to practice at least one of these confidence builders each day this week and beyond.

To your transformation!

CONFIDENCE #2

Confident people walk into a room like they own it! Their posture is good. They stand up straight and tall. They have a strong stride and walk into the room with a purpose. They look people in the eye and smile at everyone they meet, saying hello. They shake hands solidly and introduce themselves.

When you walk into a room of people, you should know your purpose. If there are only strangers in the room, make a plan to meet at least three new people. Introduce yourself. Get the other person's name and where he or she is from. Ask people questions about themselves. Or talk about the room or the day.

Smile a lot!

You will be remembered for being friendly and happy.

The more you act friendly and happy, the more you genuinely will be that way.

To your transformation!

CONFIDENCE #3

There is no leadership without confidence.

We follow people who inspire us.

Leaders have the ability to make decisions.

Leaders take risks and are not afraid to fail.

Leaders are confident in their ability to achieve and take action and make positive things happen.

We are all leaders; however, we get thwarted by our fear. We fear making mistakes or looking bad in front of others. So we become wishy-washy with our decision making and let life pass us by.

We wait for things to happen. We become afraid of making the wrong decision, so we make no decision. We become paralyzed by ourselves and our fear.

Leaders are also afraid. Everyone is afraid. The difference is that leaders push their fear aside and make decisions anyway. Leaders look their fear in the eye and say, "You can't stop me."

Leaders *act*!

Leaders are in charge. They are people in positions to make change. They are managers, principals, teachers, CEOs, CFOs, COOs, business owners, and more. Leaders lead people. Leaders are confident!

Be a leader.

To your transformation!

CONFIDENCE #4

Confidence—when you have it, it fills you up and makes you strong. Confidence is a buoy that keeps you floating in a sea of doubt. It doesn't let negativity seep inside to sink your spirits.

Negativity acts like a cement block that will sink your ship. So, you have to surround yourself with positivity to keep yourself and your team afloat.

You have a goal, a mission, and you know you can achieve what you set your mind to.

Most people who have confidence don't waste time thinking about it though. They are people of action! They know what they need to do and they do it. They have a plan and they act on it.

Your challenge this week is to take action on whatever positive change you want for yourself or others. Your action can be small or large, but be confident.

Act now.

To your transformation!

CHAPTER 16

CONNECTEDNESS

Connections *with other people affect not only the quality of our lives but also our survival.*

—Dean Ornish, physician

In Psychology 101, we learn that the feeling of belonging to a group or being *connected to others* is a basic need to be fulfilled for all people for their overall and lasting survival. This has been proven according to numerous studies and is indicated on Maslow's hierarchy of needs.

According to Maslow, there are three basic areas that need to be fulfilled for human survival. Basic or primary needs—including food, water, warmth, and shelter/safety—are the foundation of life.

Psychological needs include *connectedness* or belonging to groups/relationships that provide love and caring, as well as love for self, a sense of accomplishment, and feelings of self-worth.

The third tier of Maslow's hierarchy includes self-actualization, which is about full self-development and achievement.

Your challenge this week is to examine your *connections* in your life. This includes your connections in your family, to your friends, at work, around your neighborhood, at your place of worship, and in all areas of your life.

Make a list of where you would like to have more or better connections.

This is the first step to connecting to others—acknowledging that you want the connection!

> No man is an island, entire of itself. (John Donne, *No Man Is an Island*)

If you are feeling alone, there are some actions you can take to start connections:

- Join a club that pertains to some interest that you have.
- Write a letter to someone who you think might write back.
- Call friends or family members and ask them how they are doing and what they are up to.
- Join a social club, just for fun.
- Join a support group.
- Join a social media site.

These are just some ideas to get a start.

To your transformation!

CONNECTEDNESS #2

> *When we come from an authentic, genuine place in ourselves, our efforts to connect with people work to their fullest. Our relationships develop more easily and last longer, and we feel better about the people.*
> —Michelle Tillis Lederman, *The 11 Laws of Likability*

So, you want to be more connected to the people in your life!!

The most important thing to remember about establishing a connection and maintaining a connection with another person is to be authentic.

How do you do that? Here are some tips:

- *Be a good listener.* Give the other person *eye contact* and give them *your full attention.*

- *Paraphrase* what the person is saying so that he or she knows that you are getting what he or she is saying.
- *Ask questions* when appropriate.
- Be interested!
- *Don't be perfect.* Be vulnerable and show your imperfections. Laugh at yourself and your flaws.

    No one is perfect!

    If you pretend to be perfect, it will just make the other person feel uncomfortable because he or she isn't perfect and can't meet the expectation of perfection.
- Smile!

To your transformation!

CONNECTEDNESS #3

> *There isn't any questioning the fact that some people enter your life, at the exact point of need, want or desire—it's sometimes a coincidence and most times fate, but whatever it is, I am certain it came to make me smile.*
>
> —Nikki Rowe

People touch our lives every day when we enter a store, travel, take a class, go to work, visit friends, go to the doctor, and on and on. If we allow ourselves to be open to conversation, we allow connection.

At times, someone may seem closed off to conversation, but you never know what another person may be going through, so start the connection with the stranger on the train or in the store. Give a compliment or share a concern about the store or the train/airport. You may make a new friend. You may brighten that person's day!

Other people come and go in our lives according to reasons that are sometimes beyond our control. We reach out to them, and perhaps they are open to connecting, and perhaps they are closed off to it.

It is up to us to offer love and authenticity in order to make connections with others. It takes strength of character, courage, and unyielding love.

Reach out!

Start the conversation.
Offer love.

Connect.

To your transformation!

CHAPTER 17

CONSIDERATION

CONSIDERATION #1

Any responsible essayist or memoir writer who's writing about herself is not just saying, "Here's what happened," and opening up her diary. There needs to be consideration *of other people's feelings.*

—Faith Salie

Writing often turns into a cathartic journey for me, and this week, the topic of consideration has been an especially revealing "aha" moment.

I have always thought that I have been a kind person, loving and caring in many ways. I have tried hard to live with consideration for others. I'm always trying to do the "right" thing—the best thing for everyone involved.

The problem with "my right thing" is that it was *my* right thing. It wasn't necessarily right for everyone. It was what I thought was right. It was me being in a hurry to get things done, without consideration for other people's feelings.

There I was—being kind and considerate, but not really.

> Intensely selfish people are always very decided as to what they wish. They do not waste their energies in considering the good of others. (Ouida, *Wanda*)

There have been times in my life when people have called me selfish, closed-minded, or manipulative.

I was shocked, appalled, and hurt by these name-calling moments. I even cried and thought to myself, *No. They are wrong. I'm a good person. I'm doing good. I'm considerate and kind. I'm getting things done for everyone!"*

Interestingly, I was closed-minded to the possibility that I could be wrong.

It's funny, how life hits you in the face with your own absurdity.

While I can recognize that I am a good person at my core because my intention is pure and kind, intention does *not* carry through and become consideration for others.

So, while my intentions may have been good, I have hurt other people along my journey regardless of my love and thoughts of kindness. I was being shortsighted.

True consideration means long, careful thought given over a period of time, a long process involving a great deal of careful thought for others and their feelings; synonyms include rumination, meditation, contemplation, and reflection.

Your challenge this week is to look at your intentions and make sure you are giving your considerations enough time.

Take the time to consider everyone's feelings. If someone says you are being selfish, be willing to take a look at yourself, there may be some truth there. It doesn't mean that you are not a good person. It just might mean you are missing something in that moment.

> A moment of *consideration* often prevents a thousand apologies. (Kevin J. Anderson)

To your transformation!

CONSIDERATION #2

> *Empathy is one of humankind's prized possessions. Acts of consideration and kindness are inevitable when a person can mentally step into someone else's shoes. Even if it's just for a moment.*
>
> —Izey Victoria Odiase

It is difficult to know what another person is feeling or experiencing.

Therefore, not everyone has empathy or consideration for the feelings of another.

Nor does everyone have empathy for all people all of the time.

It is painful to have *consideration* for others when you are also experiencing pain.

There is fear involved!

If we could know what another person feels, then we would have to be more understanding.

We would have to be more compassionate, more patient, more loving—when, in reality, all we want to do is to be angry because we are hurting too.

We are sometimes more comfortable in our anger, in our sadness and/or in our pain.

As we are *considerate* of the other person(s), then we can be more open to be *considerate* of ourselves.

Feelings and emotions will be recognized and validated through our own awareness, if not by the awareness of others. With consideration comes forgiveness, for as we consider, we can be empathic, loving, and forgiving.

When we love people, we accept them and their shortcomings. Our love is unconditional, and our kindness is shown through acts of consideration over and over again.

Be forgiving if/when you fall short.

> Always remember to give yourself the kindness, compassion and *consideration* you give to others. (Miya Yamanouchi)

To your transformation!

CONSIDERATION #3

> *Good manners reflect something from inside, an innate sense of* consideration for others *and respect for self.*
> —Emily Post

There are so many things that go into having consideration for others.

Having *good manners* is just one item on the list of being considerate.

Having *patience* with other people is part of being considerate. Not everyone is as fast or as quick or as bright as you might want people to be when you want them to be so. Have patience, especially when you don't feel like it.

Staying quiet when something goes wrong or staying quiet to avoid an argument even though you are sure you are right—that is consideration!

It is sometimes more important to let a friend or coworker talk or vent. Consider their needs.

Consideration is being in tune with what other people need before they ask for it.

Give freely of yourself and your time when others need your help.

Put other people before yourself.

Consideration is intuitive. You may not always get it right, but keep trying.

Consideration is empathic. Listen to others. Walk in the other person's shoes. Understand what it feels like to be that person. Understand his or her hurt, anxiety, pain, and joy.

Consideration is forgiveness.

We need the courage to know how to apologize when necessary because we *all* mess up.

Remember to have consideration for yourself as well.

Consideration includes everyone and every person's feelings.

Consideration is love.

> *Consideration* for others is the basis of a good life, a good society. (Confucius)

To your transformation!

CHAPTER 18

CONSISTENCY

CONSISTENCY #1

It's not what we do once in a while that shapes our lives. It's what we do consistently!

—Tony Robbins

We talk about motivation and needing it to get started on projects and to work toward achieving our goals. However, it's important to realize that we need to continue our motivated action in a consistent pattern.

Consistency is important to form habits of good, positive behavior.

As Aristotle would aptly put it, "We are what we repeatedly do. Excellence then, is not an act, but a habit."

Some people believe that a new habit can be formed in twenty-one days and they sell products/programs based on this concept. However, studies have shown that behavior and habits are formed based on the difficulty of the behavior and on the individual and that new habits may take up to sixty-six days to form.

So continued motivation is essential. And consistency when it comes to working toward your goals on a daily basis is the key to success.

Your challenge is to stay consistent and to encourage and congratulate yourself and others for their efforts every day!

To your transformation!

CONSISTENCY #2

Consistent action creates consistent results.

—Christine Kane

What action are you taking today? And what results are you getting? These are the questions to be asking yourself.

Be honest with the answers to your questions! No one is judging you. Do *not judge* yourself. Be where you are and allow yourself the grace to be who you are today.

Are your actions getting you where you want to be in life? Do you want to make changes?

Are you late for work? Do you complain about your job? Do you waste time lying around on the couch when you could be taking action on your goals? (I'm guilty of this one!) Do you eat mindlessly? (Guilty again.)

There are so many negative habits that people have simply slipped into for so many different reasons that I wouldn't have the time, space, or expertise to discuss on this page. These include habits like procrastination, depression, anxiety, and fear.

The Idea, though, is to move into action in a consistent nature on a positive course to change those habits into more productive ones that will lead us all into the heroes and leaders we want to be.

Where would you like to be in one year?

What can you do today to start on the path to get there?

Clean one drawer in order to have an uncluttered home. Eat one less snack in order to lose weight. Walk around the block on your path to exercise. Research how to write a résumé, if you want a new job/career.

Start small. Put one foot in front of the other and take baby steps! Change takes time.

To your transformation!

CONSISTENCY #3

If you are persistent, you will get it. If you are consistent you will keep it.

So, you have chosen the new habits that you want to create. You are taking steps every day to make these new habits part of your new self.

Congratulations! Put a post-it note on the bathroom mirror to congratulate yourself.

Consistency is important over time in order to keep your positive habits in place—in order to maintain the habits as part of your life forever and to be the hero that you want to become. Consistency *must* be a way of life.

One tip is to find a friend who might call or text you every day to check on you and keep you motivated to succeed—keeping it positive.

Set an alarm or reminder for yourself to meet your goal(s).

Practice consistency this week for all your new, positive habits.

To your transformation!

CONSISTENCY #4

> *Success isn't always about greatness, it's about consistency.*
> *Consistent hard work equals success, then greatness will come!*
> —Dwayne Johnson

No matter what you do or who you are or where you hope to go in life, hard work is what gets you there. Combine your hard work with consistent effort, and it will equal success!

While you're working, visualize your success. Meditate to see yourself at your best, and you will be the success that you want to be. Close your eyes and see yourself in your new job, or see yourself thinner or more healthy and fit. Whatever your goal, visualize it in your mind as if you already have it.

Think positive and work toward your goal. If you slip up and fall back into old behavior, remember that the next moment and the next day is a new opportunity to succeed.

The combination of hard work, consistency, and visualization will create the you that you want to be,

See it and you will be it—consistently!

To your transformation!

CHAPTER 19

COURAGE

It takes courage *to grow up and become who you really are.*
—E. E. Cummings

I saw two of our four children today and was bursting with pride at the level of independence and success that they have achieved. My husband said, "We are so proud of the both of you—of the adults that you have become." The smiles on their faces were a testament to their happiness and reception of the compliment.

They each have successful careers, live in urban areas, and have figured out how to manage their finances in order to live alone in an expensive area. It isn't always easy, and yet they are "doing it." They are making it work—their way!

We have other children who have moved out of the area, who we are equally proud of, who have chosen other casual lifestyles and less urban areas. One lives in Vermont, and one lives in California.

Again though, our children are examples of young adults who are doing it their way. They have proven to be courageous, brave, and unafraid to make changes to get what they want in life.

Making change is scary! And that's true whether it's a small change like a haircut or buying a piece of furniture or a big change like moving to a different state.

Any change takes courage!

Your challenge this week is to make a positive change—one that you have been thinking about for a while.

Be courageous! And be the person you want to be when you grow up.

To your transformation!

COURAGE #2

> *For what it's worth: it's never too late or, in my case, too early to be whoever you want to be. There's no time limit, stop whenever you want. You can change or stay the same, there are no rules to this thing. We can make the best or the worst of it. I hope you make the best of it. And I hope you see things that startle you. I hope you feel things you never felt before. I hope you meet people with a different point of view. I hope you live a life you're proud of. If you find that you're not, I hope you have the* courage *to start all over again.*
> —Eric Roth, *The Curious Case of Benjamin Button: Story to Screenplay*

> *I may not be young but it's never too late to make a change for the better. To change my life for the positive. It just takes courage!"*
> —Cowardly Lion, speech on courage

To borrow a line from one well know group, long-term change takes place "one day at a time."

Sometimes changing something in our lives seems overwhelming and insurmountable. Approaching it with the attitude of one day at a time helps us to achieve results because we can see success daily.

Sometimes it does help to join a support group, and sometimes it doesn't. However, it always helps to have someone you can talk to about what you're experiencing—someone with whom you can share your goals and your struggles.

So, whether you are trying to lose weight, starting an exercise program, stopping a habit like biting your nails, stopping drinking or making any other change you might want to see in your life, *find* a friend or group that you can talk with to help you with your challenge. You will be more likely to meet success. There is strength in numbers.

It takes courage to change!

To your transformation!

COURAGE #3

> *When we least expect it, life sets us a challenge to test our Courage and willingness to change; at such a moment, there is no point in pretending that nothing has happened or in saying that we are not yet ready. The challenge will not wait. Life does not look back. A week is more than enough time for us to decide whether or not to accept our destiny.*
> —Paulo Coelho, *The Devil and Miss Prym*

So the lyrics to "Beautiful Boy (Darling Boy)" contain the famous Lennon quote, "Life is what happens to you while you are busy making other plans."

The line suggests that sometimes, no matter what you are doing, life just throws you a curveball with which you have to deal.

You can step up to that challenge with the courage to accept it or not and move forward or not.

I had planned to spend much of my retirement time with my sister. We had things we wanted to do and places we wanted to see. Life threw my sister the challenge of cancer. And my challenge was life after her death.

So many people in the world deal with so much tragedy and have to deal with the aftermath and rearrange their lives. They take on massive challenges. Think addiction, earthquakes, hurricanes, terrorists, and on and on, there is so much more.

Do you have the courage to meet the challenges that life throws into your path?

I believe that you do. I believe in each and every one of you. You all have the courage inside of you.

Take a deep breath and summon your courage, and it will rise to the occasion.

To your transformation!

CHAPTER 20

DECENCY

> *A* decent *life, even a short life, will always be far better than an exceptionally long-life lived-in ruin.*
>
> —Steven J. Carroll

How do you live a *decent* life?

It's simple really. There is one rule. Be kind to others.

Nothing fancy about it. No hoopla. No fanfare. Choose to be kind!

When she was little, my daughter came home from school one day. And with a serious frown upon her face, she asked, "Mom, why do *I* have to be nice all the time? Nobody else is!"

While her question and pained expression tore at my heart, I gently explained, "It's what we do, because it's the best way to be." (Of course, I made sure that what she was dealing with was something that she could manage on her own and with kindness and that it was not a bullying situation, but that's another story.)

Your challenge this week is to examine yourself and your life for your kindness. Are you stepping up to be kind to others?

Being kind doesn't mean you have to be a volunteer worker every day of the week. Simple acts of kindness can be a smile, opening a door, offering assistance, letting someone go ahead of you in line, or giving a genuine compliment.

Your kindness might just make someone's day.

Your kindness might make the difference between someone hurting him or herself or another or being decent and kind to another person instead.

Your *decency* can change the world.

To your transformation!

DECENCY #2

You cannot go on indefinitely being just an ordinary, decent egg. We must be hatched or go bad.

—C. S. Lewis

So many of us think that we are decent human beings. We go about our lives believing that we are kind and good people because we do good deeds.

Then we go home, and we snap at our children, or we lose our temper at our spouse.

Our decency, like all other traits, must be nurtured and developed. We must look after our tendency to be decent and practice our kindness and help it to grow.

How? you might ask.

Be aware of yourself!

If you are cursing or defaming others, be aware. *Speak decently* toward others. Be kind.

If you are being a jerk, own it. *Stop*! Self-correct. First, be kind to yourself in that moment. *Forgive* yourself. And then be kind to the other(s).

Become more open-minded. *Listen* to others.

Think before you act or react.

Surround yourself with people you like, so you have a *positive* influence. Do what you love. Love what you do.

Love unconditionally!

To your transformation!

DECENCY #3

I hope people remember me as a good and decent *man. And if they do, then that's success.*

—Tim Cook

The definition of *decency* is the following:

> Being kind to yourself and others
> Open-mindedness
> Loving unconditionally
> Honesty
> Having integrity
> Being true to yourself and others
> Kindness toward yourself and others
> Working hard
> Being positive
> Being a good listener
> Being optimistic
> Being authentically and comfortably *yourself*
> Do you choose to be decent?

To your transformation!

CHAPTER 21

DEVOTION

*With faith, discipline and selfless devotion to duty, there is
nothing worthwhile that you cannot achieve.*

—Muhammad Ali Jinnah

I believe that we think of God and spirituality when we hear the word
devotion. Or at least I tend to.

However, devotion means to have limitless love, loyalty, or enthusiasm
for a person, activity, or cause. It doesn't have to mean that you are devoted
to a religious cause or a spiritual person or activity.

Devotion expresses a higher level of love and commitment to your
person or cause.

As a word, it evokes a spiritual sense of duty, a higher pledge to
complete whatever task or promise you are pursuing.

Your challenge is to ask yourself if you can pledge devotion to your
goals—whether your goals are at work or at home.

Figure out what your goals are in your work and home settings.

Make a pledge of devotion (ask your higher power for some assistance).

If you are stuck, meditate on what you *love* and devote yourself to *that*
person, cause, or activity.

To succeed in your mission, you must have single-minded devotion to your goal. (A. P. J. Abdul Kalam)

To your transformation!

DEVOTION #2

True strength lies in submission, which permits one to dedicate his life, through devotion, to something beyond himself.
—Henry Miller

When you give yourself fully and completely without reservation to what you do, you will be successful.

You might be thinking, *OMG. I already work ten hours a day. I can't possible give any more!*

Working or giving yourself with devotion does not mean that you have to work harder. It does not mean you have to work longer.

It just means that you give yourself with *love.*

While you are working, love what you do. Be dedicated. Do for others as you hone your craft.

Being productive at your craft is important. Being productive in your devotion to grow as a human is essential. (Robin S. Sharma)

To your transformation!

DEVOTION #3

True love is not a strong, fiery, impetuous passion. It is, on the contrary, an element calm and deep. It looks beyond mere externals, and is attracted by qualities alone. It is wise and discriminating, and its devotion is real and abiding.
—Ellen G. White

As we continue to look at the things that we love and to find our areas of devotion, do not overlook the friends in our life who are always there for us when we need them but who we sometimes take for granted.

We *all* get so busy, especially during the holiday season, with our jobs, shopping, family obligations, and extra stress that the holiday brings. We often overlook those closest to us.

Take a look. Who is the person who is always quietly waiting to support you? Who is the person who always has your "back"? Who asks, "How can I help you?"

Be that person, for another!

Devotion is calm and enduring. Hold that person close. That is love. Trust in the power of love!

> Loyalty and devotion lead to bravery. Bravery leads to the spirit of self-sacrifice. The spirit of self-sacrifice creates trust in the power of love. (Morihei Ueshiba)

To your transformation!

CHAPTER 22

EFFECTIVENESS

EFFECTIVENESS #1

Efficiency is doing things right. Effectiveness is doing the right thing.

—Zig Ziglar

Let's say a manager is attempting to communicate more efficiently. She can accomplish her goal by using email rather than sending letters to each employee or rather than taking the time to speaking with each employee. However, a manager who's efficient with getting the message across isn't always effective and vice versa. Efficiency increases productivity and saves both time and money. However, in the process, we must be ever conscious of never losing our effectiveness.

By sending emails, this manager lost the personal touch with his or her employees. The personal interaction, which is so important for connection within the workplace, was lost. Morale will be decreased and work production will go down.

How can we be sure that we remain effective in our work, our relationships, and our lives? Take a step back and observe yourself, your team, and your surroundings. Are you happy? Are the people in your relationships, work settings, and life satisfied?

If you aren't sure of the answers to those questions, it's okay to ask. In your relationships, say, "I want to be a good friend, partner, sister, lover. How am I doing?"

Let the other person know that you want honesty. Only through honest feedback will you be able to grow and able to become effective.

At work, say, "I want to be the best employee I can be," or, "I want to be a great boss or leader here. How am I doing?"

Honest communication is key to effectiveness!

It might feel a little weird or uncomfortable at first. But try it. It will lead to enlightenment!

This is your challenge: Ask for feedback from someone this week for true effectiveness.

To your transformation!

EFFECTIVENESS #2

> *Character may almost be called the most Effective means of persuasion.*
>
> —Aristotle

We have been calling them role models—those people who we've looked up to most of our lives, those heroes we've worshiped from a far.

I'm talking about the men and women, young and old, who have had strength of spirit—those who have lifted us up from despair with their words, their actions of unselfish giving, and their courageous acts of bravery.

There have been many of them, too many to name individually. Heroes come in all shapes and sizes and from all walks of life and can be found in all the cultures of the world. Heroes are blind to differences and simply step up to do the next right thing. They see a need and they fill it with love.

True heroes give of themselves from their hearts to other living, breathing beings. Heroes are blind to any differences such as color, religion, age, gender, and so on and simply see similarities and need. Think of all of the ordinary people who have had the strength of character to *step up* in the last few weeks, months, and years and come to the aid of all of the victims of the tragedies in our country and the countries around us.

I salute them and their bravery! It only takes one brave person of character to *act*, and the rest will follow.

We are our own role models and the role models for every person with whom we come into contact.

Put your best character forward.

Be effective. Be a role model—today and every day!

To your transformation!

EFFECTIVENESS #3

> *I learned early, in sports, that to be effective—for a player to play the best he can play—is a matter of concentration and being unaware of distractions, positive or negative.*
>
> —Tom Landry

Focus is important for effectiveness!

As a student in a school setting, focus is one of the elements most impressed upon young learners.

Teachers are constantly reminding their young charges to pay attention, to listen, and to stay on the task at hand. If you are distracted as a student, you will miss an important part of the lesson and, therefore, miss the lesson as a whole.

As a driver of a car, focus is everything! The reason laws are so strict—and need to be more so to make people aware of the dangers of texting and driving, using a phone and driving, or doing anything else and driving—is that our lives depend on drivers' focus.

Just as sports players play their best without distractions and by focusing on the art and act of the game, so too is it true of our actions in everyday activities. In some cases, lack of focus can mean life or death. In some cases, our focus can make the difference between whether we achieve the honor roll or an F and whether or not we get the raise or promotion at work.

Our focus determines our effectiveness on and off the field. Minimize your distractions to optimize your effectiveness.

To your transformation!

EFFECTIVENESS #4

Effective leadership is putting first things first. Effective management is discipline, carrying it out.

—Stephen Covey

Some leaders are born, and some leaders are made through practice and hard work. Effective leaders prioritize the goals of their team. They surround themselves with team members who can carry out the tasks necessary to reach the goals of the team.

Managers assigned to the team are hardworking individuals who are disciplined and organized. Having established relationships with the team, effective managers have the ability to work with the team using communication skills and problem-solving skills. They work together to reach common goals and to advance their careers and the careers of their subordinates.

In all business settings, meetings are important to evaluate whether or not goals are being met and whether or not leaders and managers are being effective. Every employee has a yearly evaluation to assess effectiveness of performance. So, therefore, should leaders. It's the only way to know if we should readjust what we are doing—make a change to be better.

Assess yourself! Make the changes you need to be the best leader or manager you can be.

To your transformation!

EFFECTIVENESS #5

Follow effective action with quiet reflection. From the quiet reflection will come even more effective action.

—Peter Drucker

Take time for quiet reflection on what you are doing. It's a good way for self-assessment.

At the end of the day, you might want to write a journal of the day's events. Record how your solved problems or how you interacted with employees or the actions you took that day.

If you don't like to write, you might choose to meditate on the day's activities. Take fifteen minutes of quiet, uninterrupted time to be quiet and reflect on the day and your effectiveness.

Honest self-evaluation is key. Ask yourself, what could I have done differently? Better? Was it my best?

Congratulate yourself for your best action! Write down ideas that come to you for change.

Create effectiveness!

To your transformation!

CHAPTER 23

ENOUGH

ENOUGH #1

Believing in our hearts that who we are is enough is the key to a more satisfying and balanced life.

—Ellen Sue Stern

Throughout the course of my lifetime, I have spoken to "enough" people to know that thinking, *I am not enough* is pretty common. It's a thought that goes through the minds of many of us. It doesn't matter how old you are or whether or not you are just starting out on a new career or a new path in life, we all have moments of self-doubt—times when we think that we are "not enough."

There are things that have happened to us or things that we have heard over the course of time that have caused us to believe that we are not enough in one way or another.

Not being enough might mean different things to different people depending on their life experiences. We all have little voices in our heads that speak to us and tell us things. Often our little voices say, *I am not enough.*

For example, I might think that I am:

Not smart enough
Not thin enough

Not good looking enough
Not clever enough
Not able enough
Not _____ enough!

Fill in the blank based on your life experience and the little voice in *your* head.

> There are some people who through hurts do not feel they are good enough and this is a destroyer of their self-images. As a true believer of your dream, you need to see yourself as God sees you. God sees you as his own handiwork and that is pretty great to carry you through! (Israelmore Avivor, *The Great Hand Book of Quotes*)

Your challenge this week is to take the *not* out of your thinking. Change your statements to I am *enough*!

I am thin enough.
I am good-looking enough.
I am clever enough.
I am able enough.
I am _____ enough!

The truth of the matter is that *you are enough* just the way you are, regardless of what the voice in your head might be saying.

To your transformation!

ENOUGH #2

> *You alone* are enough. *You have nothing to prove to anybody.*
> —Maya Angelou

The only one you have anything to prove a thing to is to yourself!
At the end of the day, ask yourself the following questions:

- Did I do my best work?
- Did I give my best effort?
- Did I offer my best self?

If you answered no to any of those questions, you might want to take time to reflect and ask yourself *what* you want to or can do differently.

How can I change my day to make myself perform my best work, give my best effort, be my best self?

And remember, not every day has to be 100 percent flat-out energetic if you don't have it in you to give.

You have to be kind to yourself and know your limits and rejuvenate yourself as well. Just don't get caught up in comparing yourself with the "next guy.", You are your own person and your best is *your* best not his or hers. Own it. Be okay with yourself.

> At the end of the day, remind yourself that you did the best you could today, and that is *good enough.* (Lori Deschene)

To your transformation!

ENOUGH #3

> *The most important day is the day you decide you're good enough for you. It's the day you set yourself free.*
> —Brittany Josephina

One of the most freeing lessons I've ever learned was when someone told me I didn't have to be perfect.

From that comment I learned that everything I did didn't have to be flawless or errorless and that it was all right to make a mistake.

I will never forget the sense of relief that I felt. A feeling of lightness came over me like an actual weight was being lifted right off of my shoulders.

I learned the phrase, "Good enough." It doesn't have to be perfect; it just has to be good enough.

Wow! Who knew that those two words would make such a powerful impact on my life?

Instead of stressing about making everything perfect, from that day forward, I practiced making everything good enough.

Learn from your mistakes.

God made us complete! Each and every one of us was made exactly how we are—to live happily and fully. Embrace your imperfections.

> Whatever you did today is *enough*. Whatever you felt today is valid. Whatever you thought today isn't to be judged. Repeat the above each day. (Brittany Burgunder)

To your transformation!

CHAPTER 24

EVOLVING*

> *Yesterday I was clever so I wanted to change the world. Today I am wise so I am changing myself.*
>
> —Rumi

Have you ever entered into a relationship thinking, *I like this person, but he (or she) will have to change a couple of things in order for it to last?*

Have you been in relationships and thought, *we will get along when my partner stops acting that way, talking that way, being that way, or something along those lines?*

Or have you said to yourself or to them, "You just don't understand me!"

Then you go about trying to change that person or person(s) in your life so that they fit your expectation of how they should be. You try to mold them into your idea of the right sister, the right brother, the right husband, the perfect wife, the perfect friend, the perfect cousin or whatever roll the person plays in in your life.

This week's challenge is about evolving, and in order to evolve, *you* must change.

So, your challenge is to look at your relationships and ask yourself:

---

* *The pieces in this section were* inspired *by my friend A.P., with gratitude and grace.*

1. Is it me? Am I open to change? Or am I resistant to changing myself?
2. What can I do to make this relationship better?

Improve yourself first.

To your transformation!

EVOLVING #2

> *We are one. Everything in the universe is within you. Ask all from yourself.*
>
> —Rumi

Be aware that all of your relationships mirror whatever is going on inside of yourself.

If you have self-love and happiness, then you will attract love and happiness in the relationships outside of yourself.

If you have self-trust, then you will find a trustworthy partner or friend.

If you have responsibility for self, then you will attract responsible partners and friends.

All your other relationships are patterned after your relationship with yourself.

If you have relationships with others who push your "hot" buttons, or you push their "hot" buttons, pay attention to those triggers. Those are the buttons or issues that are reflected in relationships that you may need to change in yourself.

Think about it! Take a few minutes or more to reflect on how you might want to change yourself.

If someone claims that you don't understand him or her—especially a child or sibling—*stop*!

Think!

Are you listening to the person? *Really* listening to him or her? How can *you* be better?

When others speak to you, ask them to tell you more so you can really listen to them and hear them.

As you evolve, so too, will your relationships.

To your transformation!

EVOLVING #3

Let yourself be silently drawn by the strange pull of what you really love. It will not lead you astray.

—Rumi

While you are in the process of evolving, let your heart be your guide.

If you are loving certain friends or people, spend time in their company. If you find something that you love and can afford to buy it, bring it home. If you know that you love spending time outdoors, go outside and breathe in the fresh air. Take a walk. Go for a hike. Wander around in the meadow. Offer to walk a friend's dog. Ride a bike. Take a drive in the country.

If you find that you are too busy working and don't have much time but love art, shop in an art store during your lunch hour. Go to an art museum or to a craft show. Paint a picture or simply color!

Love music? Go to a concert. Listen to new tunes on the radio, in the car, at home, on your lunch break, at the gym, or wherever you go.

When you surround yourself with what you love, you will exude love. You will be excited and joyful and, yet you will also tend to be peaceful and calm.

You will be evolving into a person who is loving and loving yourself. Therefore, you will spread more love in your relationships naturally.

To your transformation!

CHAPTER 25

EXCELLENCE

EXCELLENCE #1

This week's challenge is to create action in your life that moves you toward *excellence*.

> Excellence is an art won by training and habituation. We do not act rightly because we have virtue or excellence, but we rather have those because we have acted rightly. We are what we repeatedly do. Excellence, then, is not an act but a habit. (Aristotle)

First you have to decide what excellence means to you and how you define excellence in each environment in which you spend your time.

For example, excellence in the family might look a little different than excellence in the workplace.

However, parts of some definitions of excellence will overlap from one environment to another. One definition of excellence might include:

- Accountability
- Teamwork
- Consistency
- Empowerment

Once the definition is established, then you *act* every day to meet the standards that you set for yourself and your group. Start this week by setting your standards with at least one of your groups.

To your transformation!

EXCELLENCE #2

> *The companies that survive longest are the ones that work out what they uniquely can give to the world not just growth or money but their excellence, their respect for others, or their ability to make people happy. Some call those things a soul.*
> —Charles Handy

My suggestion is to start with your family when you are looking to make a plan for success anywhere else. If your family is dysfunctional, then start with what you see as your ideal family. What are the characteristics that compose the functioning and happiness of your ideal family?

Some ideas might include:

- *Commitment.* We commit to the job and to one another. Commit to success.
- *Communication.* Everyone has a right to be heard and a turn to speak up.
- *Nonjudgment.* Everyone protects one another, even if there are disagreements. Each member has one another's back in good times and in bad times.
- *Teamwork.* We work together to get everything done because we are all part of the team. We belong equally and are all important.
- *Respect.* We are kind to one another and work with intention to get the job done regardless of differences, working with our strengths.

Take those characteristics and then apply them to other areas and groups in your life. You can expand on them in the workplace or school arena. It has been statistically shown that companies that model their work environment after a family environment thrive longer and more lucratively than other companies.

You can also choose your friends as they fit into the same circle of values and characteristics that you have chosen for your life. Then rise to the level of excellence together!

To your transformation!

EXCELLENCE #3

The secret of joy in work is contained in one word—excellence.
To know how to do something well is to enjoy it.
—Pearl Buck

So many people go to work every day and complain about their jobs. Words come out of their mouths about dreading the day, the drudgery of the work, and the pain of having to spend time inside of their work environment.

What is often overlooked is that those very people have the power to change their own existence. Their own ability to be *excellent* at their jobs can change their experience. Their own ability to think outside the box and make changes in their environments to make it more pleasant, for example, could make them employee of the month and have them stand out in the eyes of their fellow employees and employer alike.

If you do not know how to improve your skills at work, *ask* for help. Ask a friend, a colleague, or a supervisor. Email *me*. Google it. Look on YouTube. Go to the public library. A plethora of resources is available for your education and improvement.

Be creative and make your work your best! The better you become at your work, the more other opportunities will open for you, and the more you will enjoy it.

To your transformation!

EXCELLENCE #4

Happiest of birthdays to my loving husband, who strives every day to keep the excellence in our marriage! Have a wonderful day. I love you! (written on September 28, 2018)
The quality of a person's life is in direct proportion to their commitment to excellence, regardless of their chosen field of endeavor.

—Vince Lombardi

Whether your commitment to excellence is in your relationships, your family, your job, or in life in general, you will find that you will have everything you ever dreamed possible. When you devote yourself fully to something, giving 110 percent of your ability, you will derive pleasure of a job well done.

You will bask in the joy of your rewards, although they may be intangible. Happiness of an intrinsic nature can't be bought. The rewards of excellence in your relationships may be reaped with intimacy. Being authentic in your relationships and committed to the person or persons you love is definitely priceless. Have fun. Be real. Stay true to yourself and to the others in your life. Excel!

To your transformation!

EXCELLENCE #5

Desire is the key to motivation, but it's the determination and commitment to unrelenting pursuit of your goal—a commitment to Excellence—that will enable you to attain the success you seek.

—Mario Andretti

It's interesting how the topics of conversation repeat themselves in the quotes that appear at the top of the page here. Motivation, determination, and excellence are all a part of what's necessary for success.

Commitment and consistency are imperative, however, to achieve the goals that we seek. So, we can plan a family theme and design a plan to follow within our group, whether it is our actual family, our friends, our work team, or where ever. But without consistent implementation of the plan, we will not succeed. We must have *teamwork*, and consistent effort to have successful results.

If you desire the best, *you* must be the *best*! Nothing less than *excellent* is acceptable.

This is your challenge! Spread the word.

To your continued transformation!

CHAPTER 26

EXPECTATIONS

EXPECTATION(S) #1

Expectations are a loaded topic. We all have them and we all seem to manage an abundance of emotional reactions that revolve around our expectations of ourselves and others.

> I'm not in this world to live up to your expectations and
> you're not in this world to live up to mine. (Bruce Lee)

Yet, we are born into a world of expectation. Parents have a set of expectations for their baby to be a certain way at birth and hope for their child to grow into a certain type of child and, therefore, to become a certain type of young adult. Children expect parents to be nurturing, supportive, and protective. Not all parents fit into that parental mold, and not all children grow to meet the expectation of their parents.

Society has written and unwritten rules of conduct that people are expected to follow during different stages of their life. When someone does not conform to societal rules, he or she is looked upon as strange, eccentric, weird, nonconformist, or odd.

So, too, are there expectations built into a relationship. These are the things that each individual expects from the other as people enter into a combined commitment (friendship, dating, marriage or otherwise, siblings, parent/child, and so on). Every relationship comes with expectations.

When your expectations are not met, your resulting emotions are often disappointment, anger, sadness, and resentment—usually directed at the other person in the relationship. These negative emotions build up over time if left unaddressed. This is how little things add up over time and become huge relational issues.

Your challenge this week is to identify your expectations in one or more of your relationships.

1. Decide not to have expectations so that you will not be disappointed
2. Discuss your expectations with the other person so that they know what is expected, and together you can find out if these expectations are reasonable or not.
3. Adjust your expectations accordingly.
4. Have expectations for yourself, not for others—your behaviors, your reactions

To your transformation!

EXPECTATION(S) #2

> *You are your own worst enemy. If you can learn to stop expecting impossible perfection, in yourself and others, you may find the happiness that has always eluded you.*
> —Lisa Kleypas, *Love in the Afternoon*

One of the premises of Al-Anon groups and other 12-step programs is to stop having expectations of your loved ones and to start having expectations of yourself.

When a person is in recovery, it is impossible to expect him or her to be doing anything except to focus on his or her own process of sobriety and whatever that means to him or her.

You and the people who love someone who's in recovery must understand that process and have expectations for *creating your/their own happiness* and not rely on anyone else for your happiness.

When you let go of your expectations, when you accept life as it is, you're free. To hold on is to be serious and uptight. To let go is to lighten up. (Richard Carlson, *Don't Sweat the Small Stuff ... and it's all small stuff: Simple Ways to Keep the Little Things from Taking Over Your Life*)

To your transformation!

EXPECTATION(S) #3

Don't lower your expectations to meet your performance. Raise your level of performance to meet your expectations. Expect the best of yourself, and then do what is necessary to make it a reality.

—Ralph Marston

Since we are now creating expectations for ourselves, let's rise to a level of excellence, especially if excellence is one of your values.

It's your performance, *and* you do not have to be perfect. There is always room for error and humanness. But nothing less than your very best effort is acceptable.

I was inspired by a friend of mine who recently achieved her best on a graduate exam. Being proud of her ancestry and proud of her future at the same time, she put everything she had into becoming a licensed social worker. She raised her performance to meet her expectation of excellence. Nothing less would do for her because she wanted to be able to show herself that she could do it. She was just an awesome inspiration for others!

There might be failures along the way to success. That's okay. If you falter and fail, be kind; know that's normal and human. You just need to pick yourself up and brush yourself off when you fall. Get back up and move forward again toward success.

I failed my first two college courses after I graduated from high school, although not too many people know that (they know now).

I was not a great student; I was unfocused and confused. I thought that college was not for me, so I dropped out. It took me a while before I decided to go back to get a degree. And, finally, I did succeed, becoming the first person in my family to graduate from college.

Failure is part of the learning process—learning about life and learning about yourself.

Set your expectations for yourself to be your best self! Raise yourself up, up, *up*.

To your transformation!

> Set the standard! *Stop expecting others to show you love, acceptance, commitment, & respect when you don't even show that to yourself.*
> —Steve Maraboli, *Unapologetically You: Reflections on Life and the Human Experience*

CHAPTER 27

FAITH

FAITH #1

None of us knows what might happen even the next minute, yet still we go forward. Because we trust, because we have faith.

—Paulo Coelho

Faith is believing in something even when you can't see it.

Faith is believing in something stronger than yourself.

It's believing something can be a higher power—God if you will. *But it can be anything!* You can have faith in another person. You can have faith in a thing.

Faith leads you toward something—toward something greater and stronger than yourself.

You have to give up control and the idea of perfect and have faith if you want certain things in life.

Twelve years ago, today, I was nervous and anxious. But I had faith. I had faith in love and faith in another person to be the things that I thought were possible.

I was not looking to get married "again." Both my partner and I were thinking that marriage was the last thing we should do, but we took that leap of "faith." We had faith in ourselves and faith in each other.

Our union has surpassed my imagination by growing our partnership and commitment beyond what I ever thought possible. While it hasn't always been easy, we have found harmony together, creating perfection in our imperfect world as we go.

So, if your life is crazy and less than what you want it to be, your challenge this week is to simply let go of your ideas of perfection and have *faith*.

Have faith that what is meant to be for you and your life is coming.

Your perfection is created by the actions you take every day. So, stop waiting for things to be perfect. They won't be. Act now!

To your transformation!

> *Life is full of happiness and tears; be strong and have* faith.
> —Kareena Kapoor Khan

And to my husband, I am forever grateful for you and your love. Happy anniversary! (written February 18, 2019)

FAITH #2

> *Sometimes beautiful things come into our lives out of nowhere. We can't always understand them, but we have to trust in them. I know you want to question everything, but sometimes it pays to just have a little faith.*
> —Lauren Kate

Sometimes good things happen in our lives, and sometimes, bad things happen in our lives. Either way, we often have difficulty dealing with what happens,, good or bad.

We try to understand the reasons behind what has happened and there never seems to be a good explanation. This is when having faith comes in handy.

It's not necessary to understand the reasons behind what happens in life. It's useless to beat our heads against the proverbial wall trying to make sense of things.

You may be asking, How? How do I live with this? How do I have faith? How do I believe that life will just happen the way it's supposed to happen?

Well, first, practice meditation or prayer or quiet moments of just letting go.

Let go of the idea that you are in control.

There is a divine presence in the universe that is greater than ourselves, more powerful than anything that we can imagine.

> None of us knows what might happen even the next minute, yet still we go forward. Because we trust. Because we have Faith. (Paulo Coelho)

When you drive your car, you have faith that the other drivers in the other cars will follow the same rules of the road that you are following. When you stop and you drive defensively, you also have faith that the other driver will stop at the red light or stop sign. You have faith that the other drivers will stay on their side of the road.

When you go to sleep at night, you have faith that you will wake up in the morning.

> To one who has faith, no explanation is necessary. To one without faith, no explanation is possible. (Thomas Aquinas)

To your transformation!

FAITH #3

> Faith *is a knowledge within the heart, beyond the reach of proof.*
>
> —Khalil Gibran

It is not an accident that faith is said to come from the heart.

Nor is it a mistake that faith comes first in the trio of virtues in the New Testament—faith, hope, and charity (love).

Without faith, life is empty and wrought with nothing.

Faith can be in multiple areas of your choosing:

- Faith in God, as you understand Him or Her.
- Faith in a higher power.
- Faith in yourself.
  Believe in yourself! Have faith in your abilities! Without a humble but reasonable confidence in your own powers you cannot be successful or happy. (Norman Vincent Peale)
- Faith in another person or in people.
- Faith in an institution or in a place.

Having faith has much to do with your attitude and outlook on life in general.

A positive outlook shows that you have faith in life itself.

> Optimism is the faith that leads to achievement. Nothing can be done without hope and confidence. (Helen Keller)

Continue to develop your faith every day to expand your life's journey.

Meditate.

Breathe.

Set your intention for your life and let it happen.

Take actions in tune with your intentions.

To your transformation!

> *Faith makes all things possible ... love makes all things easy.*
> —Dwight L. Moody

CHAPTER 28

FEARLESSNESS

What would you do if you weren't afraid?
—Spencer Johnson, *Who Moved My Cheese?*

What would you do if you weren't afraid?

Interesting question, isn't it?

Would you learn to fly a plane?
Would you tell the truth?
Would you apologize to a friend or family member?
Would you forgive someone a past transgression?
Would you ask someone out?
Would you look for a new job?
Would you sing in public places, on stage?
Would you go to school or change careers altogether?
Would you call someone who you haven't spoken to in ten years due to a falling out?

Start a business, buy a home, make an investment, travel, learn a new skill, talk to strangers?

The list is endless!

Fears—everyone has them. Ever present, fears can be immobilizing.

103

They can be big or small, but whatever their, size they loom large in our hearts and minds and can be overpowering.

Fears stop us from becoming and stop us from being who we are.

Some fears are real—like the fear of sharks if you are swimming in shark infested water.

Some fears are imagined—like the fear you might have of not being smart enough or good-looking enough or simply not being enough. There is a little voice in your head telling you to be afraid.

Your challenge this week is to face your fears.

Make a list of what they are and decide if they are real fears or imagined. If your fear(s) are imagined, can you help yourself overcome them?

> I feel myself becoming the fearless person I have dreamt of being. Have I arrived? No. But I'm constantly evolving and challenging myself to be unafraid to make mistakes. (Janelle Monae)

To your transformation!

FEARLESSNESS #2

> *F-E-A-R has two meanings: "Forget Everything and Run" or "Face Everything and Rise." The choice is yours.*
>
> —Zig Ziglar

The easy path is the one we often take even though we dislike running. We see something we don't like or something that frightens us, and we run away. We might complain that it's too hard, or we can't do it. We close our eyes and turn away.

Then we experience secondary feelings, or what I like to call sidetracked emotions. We get depressed, or we experience lack of motivation in our daily lives. We might start to overeat. We might drink too much. We might exhibit behaviors of anger toward others and/or ourselves.

These emotions grow and overcome us because we are really angry with ourselves for not confronting our fear. These secondary behaviors occur because we didn't address our initial fear—whatever it was.

I was afraid to write this blog, so I engaged in many avoidant activities. Some were unhealthy like overeating, watching TV, napping, and yelling at my husband. Some were good like cleaning my closets or walking the dog. None confronted my fear.

Other fears that we may encounter during our lives are multiple. I was afraid to tell my boss that I was responsible for the problem at the office. I was fearful to talk to my spouse about the fact that I was feeling unhappy. I was afraid to speak up at the meeting because colleagues might think that I'm stupid.

When you're afraid, you cannot act. That is the simple truth. The voice inside your head tells you loudly and clearly, *No. Stop. It's too scary. You cannot do that!*

However, you can confront your fear and see it for what it is— *imaginary*. Act as if you are brave and *un*afraid. Deal with the fear and the voice inside your head directly—tell it to *go away*! You can overcome it and make your fears subside.

> Be exactly who you are. [You are enough.] You can fit in any space you see yourself in. Be fearless. (Dawn Richard)

To your transformation!

FEARLESSNESS #3

> *Becoming fearless isn't the point. That's impossible. It's learning how to control your fear, and how to be free from it.*
> —Veronica Roth

Even though the theme here is fearlessness, there is no such thing as being completely without fear. Even the most courageous among us have some level of fear.

> Bravely overcoming one small fear gives you the courage to take on the next. (Daisaku Ikeda)

We will always have fears to overcome. That's what life is about and what being human is about. It takes thought and courage to face our fears and to not let them stop us from living productive and full lives.

It's important to remember two things on your journey while dealing with and overcoming your fears. First, surround yourself with people who love and support you. During times of stress, you will find courage from them.

Second, meditate, and rely on your higher power. You are never alone when you stop to think about the support you receive from your higher power, God, or whatever that means to you.

> Face your fears and doubts, and new worlds will open to
> you. (Robert Kiyosaki)

To your transformation!

CHAPTER 29

FORGIVENESS

*The truth is, unless you let go, unless you forgive yourself,
unless you forgive the situation, unless you realize that the
situation is over, you cannot move forward.*
> —Steve Maraboli, *Unapologetically You:
> Reflections on Life and the Human Experience*

*Let's face it we make mistakes! Who said, "To err is human,
to forgive divine"?*
> —Alexander Pope, "An Essay on Criticism")

We all need a little divinity to emanate from within ourselves in order to
forgive ourselves.

We wake up in the morning and look in the mirror and see every
blemish, every hair that is out of place, every wrinkle, every dimple or fat
roll. We criticize ourselves for each and every imperfection.

We blame ourselves for our past mistakes, our past lapses of good
judgment, and our poor decisions. We ask ourselves, why did I stay out so
late? Why did I eat that chocolate cake? Why did I lie? Why didn't I do
better? Why, Why, why?

Then we beat ourselves up—in our minds—over and over, again and
again for those mistakes!

Forgiveness is key! It is easier to forgive others than to forgive ourselves, but, in order to live our best life, it is *so* important to forgive ourselves all of our transgressions.

In order to forgive ourselves, we must realize that life is a journey, and we are learning along the way. Being perfect is not something we should aspire to. Rather, to be human and to accept ourselves for who we are and accept others is the goal to achieve.

You (and I) are pretty great just the way *we* are! As long as we're learning from our mistakes, we're growing, and our journey is continuing. Hopefully we are having fun along the way.

Your challenge is to accept yourself, mistakes and all. Forgive yourself! Forgive someone else! Enjoy your journey.

To your continued transformation!

FORGIVENESS #2

> *I think that if God forgives us, we must forgive ourselves. Otherwise, it is almost like setting up ourselves as a higher tribunal than Him.*
>
> —C. S. Lewis

Whatever your spiritual beliefs, it is important to remember that forgiveness is the key to have forward movement. Without forgiveness, we easily get stuck in the past. We dwell in the actions of past mistakes and punish ourselves or others for prior actions.

We could get argumentative and/or philosophical and say that people don't change. The truth is that people *can* and *do* change.

Behavior, whether it is good or bad, is just a momentary action.

People do have isolated lapses of judgment—something that takes place in one place and time. Someone's entire character isn't necessarily defined by one or two incidents.

A person can change his or her behavior. People can redefine their moral codes and even their values. A person can change his or her thoughts, and people can change their feelings. Which changes first, however, thoughts, feelings, or behavior, is up for a much longer discussion.

But, if you have had a lapse of behavior and done something, you're not proud of, you need to find a way to forgive yourself so that you can move forward.

Or if you've experienced a failure of some type that you have difficulty accepting, find the lesson in it.

Embrace forgiveness! *And* move forward.

To your transformation!

FORGIVENESS #3

> *True forgiveness is when you can say, "Thank you for that experience."*
>
> —Oprah Winfrey

How do you forgive yourself?

1. Put it in the past where it belongs. Whatever happened, happened. You can't change it. Apologize in person or in a letter—whatever format works. Move forward.
2. Identify your moral code and life values and live by them every day.
3. Learn from your mistakes and/or failures. Find the lesson(s). Embrace the lesson(s).
4. Exercise—build physical strength.
5. Build inner strength
6. Surround yourself with supportive people
7. Have faith that you are where you are supposed to Be *now*—be grateful!
8. Be grateful for second chances. Be grateful for your life *now*.

> We are told that people stay in love because of chemistry, or because they remain intrigued with each other, because of many kindnesses, because of luck. ... Part of it has got to be forgiveness and gratefulness. (Ellen Goodman)

"Heart of the Matter" by the Eagles is one of my favorite songs. If I could put the entire version in song here in the book, I would. I encourage everyone to take a moment to listen to it because, while all the words may not be pertinent to our circumstances, the chorus reminds us to forgive ourselves.

Practice forgiveness.

To your transformation!

CHAPTER 30

FRIENDSHIP

Be slow to fall into friendship; but when thou art in, continue firm and constant.

—Socrates

I chose the topic of friendship this week because I was reading a book by Ron Hall and Denver Moore based on their friendship and life story, *Same Kind of Different as Me*. In the book, Mr. Moore compares friendship to fishing. He didn't want to be friends if the friendship was going to be similar to the catch-and-release fishing program. Rather his idea of friendship was based on catch-and-keep, forever.

His idea of friendship runs deeply close to my own. When I make a friend, it is forever. I cherish my friends and hold them, their secrets, their needs and desires, and their lives close to my heart for life. There is almost nothing that a friend could ask me that I would not do. I give of myself freely.

When distance separates me from my friend, which it inevitably does, due to the circumstances of life, our friendship continues without the need to speak of it.

When we meet again, it's like no time has passed, even though it may have been one year or ten. Sometimes my friend is surprised by this natural occurrence of friendship and renewed connection, but it never surprises me, because it just seems like love is normal between us. When I love a friend, I love unconditionally and completely. We don't have to see one another regularly for love to be present.

I know other people who are similar to myself when it comes to their friends. When we are lucky enough to find one another, we become friends in kind.

> You can make more friends in two months by becoming interested in other people than you can in two years by trying to get other people interested in you. (Dale Carnegie)

I will admit that I have not always been the best of friends nor have I always been the kindest. Over the years, I have had the driving purpose to learn from my mistakes and to be a better friend every day.

Your challenge this week is to consider how you can be a better friend to the friends you have.

Make a *call* to those friends you haven't spoken to in a while. Let them know you're thinking of them. Send them your love. Send an *email*. Send a quick *text* with a loving message.

It doesn't take much to let a friend know that you love him or her. Whether they are near or far, all friends need to be reminded that you love them.

To your transformation!

> *One loyal friend is worth ten thousand relatives.*
>
> —Euripides

FRIENDSHIP #2

> *Wishing to be friends is quick work, but friendship is a slow-ripening fruit.*
>
> —Aristotle

Being a friend and having a friend has been a mainstay of life since the beginning of time. Researching the topic and reading about the opinions of the founding fathers of philosophy shows not much has changed.

There are basically, *three types of friends* in life, as determined in 384 BC by Aristotle.

The first type is a friend of utility, one based on use. Each person gets something from the other, quid pro quo. These types of friendships, found in the workplace among colleagues, in school settings among classmates, or on some common ground, often expire when the setting changes.

The second type of friendship is based on the pleasure principle. When two or more people have a common interest and get together to share this pleasure, they may become friends. Some examples would be friendships formed in clubs with interests such as bicycle tour groups, yoga groups, book clubs, ski clubs, jazz or music groups, and so on. If interest in these activities decline or if one or more members stop being able to attend, then these friendships may also cease to exist.

The third type of friend is one of "the good." This is the most important among the three types of friendships, as these types of relationships are based on respect, appreciation of each other's qualities, and a strong will to aid and assist the other person because one recognizes the other's greatness.

Friendships of the third type have the potential to last forever. These friendships are based on unconditional love and acceptance of the other person.

Of course, there can be an overlap of one type of friendship into another. By this, I mean you can meet someone in a certain setting, such as school or work; develop a friendship of utility; and expand into a relationship of "the good" as you bond and create a deeper understanding of one another.

Look at your friendships and determine if they are satisfactory to you. Are your friendships the type and quality of relationships that you want them to be? You have the ability to change your friendships by investing yourself and investing your time.

To have a friend, you must be a friend. (unknown)

To your transformation!

Some of the biggest challenges in relationships come from the fact that most people enter a relationship in order to get something: they're trying to find someone who's going to make them feel good. In reality, the only way a relationship will last is if you see your relationship as a place that you go to give; and not a place that you go to take.

—Anthony Robbins

FRIENDSHIP #3

A friend is one that knows you as you are, understands where you have been, accepts what you have become, and still, gently allows you to grow.

—William Shakespeare

I am forever grateful for my true friends—those people who know all of my faults and mistakes and love me in spite of everything that I have done and in spite of or because of everything I have been.

My husband is one of those people. In fact, he is on the top of my friendship list.

I will admit that I was afraid to tell him some of the things I had done in my life. I had the normal amount of fear. Maybe I had more fear than the normal amount. Who knows? But the point is, through my fear or in spite of my fear, I have been honest with my husband because we are friends.

Our friendship has grown because of our honesty and because of our ability to love and accept one another.

People actually ask us what do we have in common? How do we stay married? How are we compatible?

Here is my answer: My husband is my best friend. He is my *good friend*, who I respect and admire. We encourage one another to grow and to be our best selves, whether that is together or apart. *And* I will venture to say that he feels the same way about me.

We communicate honestly and rely on one another for conversation about life. Our friendship is one that will last forever. We will find activities to do together for fun in our spare time, but our friendship is solid.

It is not lack of love, but a lack of friendship that makes unhappy marriages. (Friedrich Nietzsche)

Whether you find your friends in your marriage, your family, your immediate social circle, your church, or your grocery store, it doesn't matter. Cherish them!

Of all possessions a friend is the most precious. (Herodotus)

To your transformation!

CHAPTER 31

GENEROSITY

GENEROSITY #1

"A fight is going on inside me," said an old man to his son.
"It is a terrible fight between two wolves.
"One wolf is evil. He is anger, envy, sorrow, regret,
greed, arrogance, self-pity, guilt, resentment,
inferiority, lies, false pride, superiority, and ego.
"The other wolf is good. He is joy, peace, love, hope,
serenity, humility, kindness, benevolence, empathy,
generosity, *truth, compassion and faith.*
"The same fight is going on inside you."
The son thought about it for a minute and
then asked, "Which wolf will win?"
The old man replied simply, "The one you feed."
—Wendy Mass, *Jeremy Fink and the Meaning of Life*

Your challenge this week is to feed the good wolf.

Be generous.

To your transformation!

GENEROSITY #2

Holiday Gift Suggestions:
To your enemy, forgiveness.
To an opponent, tolerance.
To a friend, your heart.
To a customer, service.
To All, charity.
To every child, a good example.
To yourself, respect.

—Oren Arnold

In the Spirit of generosity
offer a hand to a stranger,
peace to someone that you have been arguing or fighting
with,
Food to the hungry,
Money to the poor,
Kindness to the downtrodden.
A generous spirit will make you a happier person.

Remember how happy Ebenezer Scrooge became when he finally let go of his miserly ways and became generous and openhearted? His face took on a glowing light and his heart soared with love.

Your heart will also soar as you, too, offer generosity to others.

A giving spirit is a learned habit. The more you practice, the easier it becomes.

To your transformation!

GENEROSITY #3

Giving is the master key to success, in all applications of human life.

—Bryant McGill

Granted, we are not all in a position to give money or gifts. We all *are* in the position to give kindness and to offer a helping hand to others.

So in lieu of tangible gifts, give the gift of time. Give time spent with a grandparent or elderly relative, friend or neighbor. Give time running an errand for a friend with small children or babysitting so Mom can take some time for herself.

Remember friends who have suffered a loss recently and stop by for a visit or send a note to let them know that you are thinking about them.

Bake a treat for a neighbor or friend.

Invite single friends and neighbors over to be part of family get-togethers. No one needs to be alone all the time.

Be creative.

Be thoughtful.

Be generous with your time.

To your transformation!

***

And for those of us on the receiving end of generosity:

> In the end, though, maybe we must all give up trying to pay back the people in this world who sustain our lives. In the end, maybe it's wiser to surrender before the miraculous scope of human *generosity* and to just keep saying thank you, forever and sincerely, for as long as we have voices. (Elizabeth Gilbert, *Eat, Pray, Love: One Woman's Search for Everything Across Italy, India and Indonesia*)

> No one has ever become poor by giving. (Anne Frank)

Note: These pieces on generosity were originally written during the holiday season, but the spirit of generosity can be with us throughout the year.

CHAPTER 32

GIVING

Giving is an expression of gratitude for our blessings.
—Laura Arrillaga-Andreessen

As we enter this holiday season,* let us be mindful of our blessings and be grateful for what we have and give to others in any way that we can.

Your challenge this week is to think of ways you can give to others and then take action, be kind, and be giving.

You can be giving of heart.

You can be giving of spirit.

You can be giving of time.

You can be giving of love.

Some ideas include:

- Donate time and/or money to a shelter for animals.
- Donate time and/or money to a shelter for the homeless.
- Donate clothes to any center that is close to your home or close to your heart.
- Collect toys for children—Toys for Tots or children in the hospital or Ronald McDonald House.

---

* While these pieces on giving were originally written in November, giving is not exclusively done in the month of November. Any time is the right time to give!

- Give someone a ride to work.
- Help someone with a task—a family member or friend.
- Send an encouraging note to someone who is struggling.
- Smile at the stranger on the bus/train.
- Buy a coffee for someone.
- Call a long-lost relative or friend.
- Forgive someone.

No act of giving is too small.

> Remember that the happiest people are not those getting more, but those *giving* more. (H. Jackson Brown, Jr.)

To your transformation!

GIVING #2

> *Kindness in words creates confidence. Kindness in thinking creates profoundness. Kindness in* giving *creates love.*
> —Lao Tzu

There are multiple ways to be giving.

Sometimes you give because you are forced into it by others or by circumstances. And, sometimes you give because you feel obligated to do so. These situations of giving do not produce love. Only giving through kindness produces love.

When you give because you want to give purely for the sake of giving your heart, your time, your money, or your love, do you produce love? Look at your motivation for giving and ask yourself, why am I giving? Is it for me? Is it for others? Am I giving freely and purely?

When you give for others without an agenda, you will produce love for yourself and for others.

To your transformation!

GIVING #3

You give but little when you give of your possessions.
It is when you give of yourself that you truly give.
—Kahlil Gibran, *The Prophet*

The easiest giving is that of giving money or things to others. When you give your time and effort to others, that is when you are really making a difference and really giving of yourself.

That doesn't mean do not give your money or donate things to others if that is the only way that you can help. Help in every way that you can! But give of yourself as often as you can too.

Listen to others when they need to talk to someone. Give of your time. Give someone a helping hand with a task or help with a chore that might be difficult for someone.

Give especially when someone asks for help. Recognize that it was difficult for the person to ask for help, so give your assistance when you can.

You might think that you are too busy. You might say that you have too much to do already and can't possibly give time or help to another. You might think that there is just no more time in your day.

However, it is in giving that we receive the full bounty and abundance of life.

Those who are happiest are those who do the most for others. (Booker T. Washington)

To your transformation!

CHAPTER 33

GIVING SPACE

GIVING SPACE #1

Let there be spaces in your togetherness, *and let
the winds of the heavens dance between you.
Love one another but make not a bond of love: Let it
rather be a moving sea between the shores of your souls.
Fill each other's cup but drink not from one cup.
Give one another of your bread but
eat not from the same loaf.
Sing and dance together and be joyous,
but let each one of you be alone,
Even as the strings of a lute are alone though
they quiver with the same music.
Give your hearts, but not into each other's keeping.
For only the hand of Life can contain your hearts.
And* stand together, yet not too near together*: For
the pillars of the temple stand apart, and the oak tree
and the cypress grow not in each other's shadow.*
—Kahlil Gibran, *The Prophet*

It is in the wanting to be together that a relationship is kept strong and
that the individuals within it are kept strong as well.

Maintaining respect for each other as individuals and supporting one another's growth and development is important.

Encouraging each person in the relationship to follow his or her dreams and to pursue his or her interests, so that both can be their best selves is paramount for both persons.

Your challenge: Are you giving *yourself* enough space to grow in your relationships? Are you *getting* enough space to grow? Are you *giving* enough space to those you love?

Are you encouraging growth? Strength? Dreams? For yourself and for your partner?

There is a difference between giving space and being distant. When you give space, you are actively aware of what the other person wants, what he or she is interested in, and what his or her dreams and goals are. You encourage the other to act on his or her dreams. You find ways to help your partner, if you can, *and* inspire him or her to act on his or her intentions. If your partner has anxiety to act on his or her own then you gently push him or her into action.

It is your job to do what is best for yourself and to do what is best for your partner as well.

To your transformation!

GIVING SPACE #2

> *Whether it is a friendship or a relationship, all bonds are built on trust. Without it, you have nothing.*
>
> —Unknown

Sometimes when we fall in love or fall in "like" with another person, we do so at the exclusion of all others and all things. We become blinded by our need or desire to be with that person.

Even in friendships, we at times become so entranced by our excitement and joy of being with these other people, we forget to give ourselves the time and space that we need to develop and grow. We may even become envious or jealous of the time that the other person spends doing other things, either alone or with others that do not include us.

We start doubting ourselves and we start to doubt the other person and intentions toward us.

Do they really like us?

Do they really love us?

Can we count on them to be our friend?

Only time will be the true indicator of whether or not your friend or lover will be the person who stands by your side through the good times and the bad. You have to *trust* that the other person will be there for you, and you in turn have to be there for him or her.

There is an old adage that says, "in order to get the right friends in your life, you have to *be* the right friend first!" Like usually attracts like—which means you will attract the kind of person you want in your life by acting and being that kind of person yourself.

You are 100 percent responsible for what you attract into your life! When you act needy and clingy and try to hold on tightly to another person you actually end up pushing them away, because people seek to reach out, spread their wings, and grow.

Like the branches of a tree that reach out from the foundation of its trunk, when the foundation of your relationship is strong and trusting, the rest of your being branches out to develop and grow, sprouting luscious leaves of life and bountiful flowers of possibility.

When you are in a relationship, you will branch out in ways that either bring you closer together or take you farther apart. Your choices will determine whether or not you are meant to be together as a couple, as friends for the long haul, or for just a short time.

> We need to give each other the *space* to grow, to be ourselves, to exercise our diversity. We need to give each other space so that we may both give and receive such beautiful things as ideas, openness, dignity, joy, healing, and inclusion. (Max de Pree)

To your transformation!

GIVING SPACE #3

The greatest relationships are the ones you never expected to be in.

—Unknown

Time and again, the relationships about which you hear people say, "I would have never seen them together," are the best ones. These are the relationships where people have let go of the unrealistic images we have of our ideal person and opened themselves to possibilities.

Sometimes we need to give ourselves space—space to allow things to be different than what we thought they should be or what our original perception may have been.

We are brought up a certain way. We go to school, and when we become adults, we choose to live in an area we like. It may or may not be an area that is near where we grew up. Life changes. So why can't we? Why can't we let go of that image of what perfect is supposed to look like?

First, get an image in your mind of what that perfect image is to you. Get it clear in your mind. What is good about it? What do you like? What do you not like as much? What can you let go of?

Give yourself the space to imagine a new possibility!

Choose three to five words that describe your perfect relationship, or job, living situation. What would it look like? Feel like? What needs would be met?

Now imagine a new possibility—in your relationship, in a career, in a living situation. Imagine away.

Hold onto your words! You have the ability to create whatever you have imagined/created.

To your transformation!

CHAPTER 34

GRACIOUS

GRACIOUS #1

When I hear the word *gracious*, it seems like a feminine word, a word that comes with a female hostess who gently and lovingly greets her guests as they enter her home for the holidays. She welcomes them all with equal kindness and love, calmly offering each and every one beverages and food and the warmth and comfort of her home.

However, being gracious is a way of being for everyone.

> If a man be *gracious* and courteous to strangers, it shows
> he is a citizen of the world. (Francis Bacon)

The actual definition of being gracious includes being kind, courteous, pleasant, merciful, compassionate, polite, and calm. It's offering comfort to others *and* behaving this way, even when you don't feel like it!

Your challenge this week is to *think* about the definition of what it means to be gracious. Then take a personal inventory of how gracious you are and up your "gracious game."

> Every little *gracious* act adds to the quotient of grace in
> the world—how gracious can you be today? All of you
> are connected—all of us are connected—we are all One
> being—breathing, living, light." (Angie Karan)

To your transformation!

GRACIOUS #2

God is Love—He is gracious *and forgives.*

—Jim George

There are so many pearls of wisdom written in the Bible and elsewhere about God. In Joel 2:13 (KJV), we read, "And turn unto the Lord your God: for he is gracious and merciful, slow to anger, and of great kindness."

I am not a particularly religious person, but for the purposes of graciousness, I think that it is important to point out that, whatever you believe in as a higher power, they are all gracious.

So then, by nature of the law of the universe, we should be gracious.

Buddha is referred to as compassionate and merciful. In Hinduism, your actions create your karma, and your karma determines your destiny.

In Islam, God (called Allah in Arabic) is described as "Al-Rahman Al-Rahim," "the Most *Gracious*, the Most Merciful" in reference to God's infinite mercy toward His creatures.

> [All] praise is [due] to Allah, Lord of the worlds—the Most Gracious, the Most Merciful. (Al-Fatihah 1:2–3)

Being gracious includes forgiveness, start by forgiving yourself and then forgiving others.

> Not only is forgiveness the most tender part of love, it is always a choice and always accompanied by unconditional love. May you always be forgiving, kind and *gracious*, especially when others are undeserving. (Rhonda Louise Robbins)

To your transformation!

GRACIOUS #3

There is hardly a more gracious *gift that we can offer somebody than to accept them fully, to love them almost despite themselves.*

—Elizabeth Gilbert

During this season especially,* and throughout the year ahead, offer the gift of friendship to those we already know and love *and* to those we meet for the first time.

You may not like everything about everyone you meet or know, but that's all right. They may not like everything about you either.

Be gracious! Be patient, calm, and kind.

> Because of a friend, life is a little stronger, fuller, more *gracious* thing for the friend's existence, whether he be near or far. If the friend is close at hand, that is best; but if he is far away, he still is there to think of, to wonder about, to hear from, to write to, to share life and experience with, to serve, to honor, to admire, to love. (A C Benson)

To your transformation!

---

* Originally written December 2018.

CHAPTER 35

GRATITUDE

GRATITUDE #1

Develop an attitude of gratitude, and give thanks for everything that happens to you, knowing that every step forward is a step toward achieving something bigger and better than your current situation.

—Brian Tracy

Don't look back! Give thanks for everything that happens to you on your journey of life because it is the journey that is creating your *best* life.

Even though sometimes on your life's journey you might want to throw in the proverbial towel and quit or you might want to throw your hands up and run in the opposite direction, because life can be difficult and sometimes it is hard to keep going.

Allow yourself a good cry when things feel out of control or when things seem to not be going the way you want them to be going.

Just remember to be grateful for where you are at the moment.

Be grateful for the people in your life.

Be grateful for the things in your life, however small.

Everything in your path and everyone on your journey teaches you something. Look for the lesson.

If you don't see it, I encourage you to look deeper, look harder, and look longer until you find it.

The lessons learned are all there inside of you.

Your challenge this week is to look for the lessons that you have learned from the things that have happened in your life lately—good and bad.

Look for the lessons that you have learned from the people in your life—both the positive experiences and the negative experiences.

Be grateful for those lessons.

> If you concentrate on finding whatever is good in every situation, you will discover that your life will suddenly be filled with gratitude, a feeling that nurtures the soul. (Rabbi Harold Kushner)

To your transformation!

GRATITUDE #2

> *He is a wise man who does not grieve for the things which he has not, but rejoices for those which he has.*
>
> —Epictetus

Take a mental inventory of what you have at the beginning of this holiday season.* You can write things down if you like. It's the reverse of making a list for Santa and asking for the things that you want.

You will be thanking yourself, Santa, your parents, the universe, and God for bringing you all the things that you already have.

> Be Thankful for what you have; you'll end up having more. If you concentrate on what you don't have, you will never, ever have enough. (Oprah Winfrey)

While you are thinking of the things that you wish you had, the things that you want, make a list of all of the things that you already have.

One of the best ways to be grateful is to keep a gratitude journal. Write down at least one thing that you are grateful for every day. It can be very simple, very small or large; it doesn't matter.

---

* Originally written November 2018.

You can be grateful for the kindness of a stranger, the love of a friend, the warmth of your cup of tea, the hugs from your dog or cat, an encouraging note/text from someone.

Be grateful for the people in your life. Nurture those relationships.

> *Gratitude* unlocks the fullness of life. It turns what we have into enough, and more. It turns denial into acceptance, chaos into order, confusion into clarity. It can turn a meal into a feast, a house into a home, a stranger into a friend. (Melody Beattie)

To your transformation!

GRATITUDE #3

> *Two kinds of gratitude: The sudden kind we feel for what we take; the larger kind we feel for what we give.*
> —Edwin Arlington Robinson

We are taught to be grateful for everything we get in life when we are taught manners and say thank you after receiving everything we "get."

However, our manners become ingrained in us and we say, "Thank you," without even thinking about what it means after a while. Therefore, it loses its meaning and becomes automatic word rush.

Yet, it is still polite to say, "Thank you," for receiving, even though we do it without much thought.

Still, we become hesitant to allow others to help us, and we do not want to accept the gifts of giving from others. We seem to have become a society of people who want to prove that we can do it all on our own. We want to prove that we can become rich, powerful, and strong independently of others.

I feel sad about that for a few reasons. First, helping others is an honor and a privilege. It generally makes a giver feel grateful that he or she is able to do something good for another person.

Second, when we do not accept help, we deny another person that experience of feeling grateful to be able to give help.

Third, and most importantly:

> God has given us two hands: one to receive with, the other to give with. (Billy Graham)

To your transformation!

CHAPTER 36

GROWTH

> *Change and* growth *take place when a person has risked himself and dares to become involved with experimenting with his own life.*
>
> —Herbert Otto

Life is a series of changes that lead us on a journey of becoming. The path that we take is based on our choices.

Our choices determine our levels of happiness, and our process is often one of self-discovery and *growth*.

Aristotle said that we are what we frequently do. If we do the same things repeatedly that make us miserable or unhappy, then that is what we are. If we spend our time doing loving and joyous activities, then that is what we are.

Think about which category you fall into—miserable and unhappy or loving and joyous. Which category do you want to be living in?

Would you be willing to try an experiment in your life to live in the category that you prefer? What would it take for you to change and grow? Time? Money? Support?

Think about it!

Twenty years from now you will be more disappointed
by the things that you didn't do than by the ones you did
do. (Mark Twain)

Your challenge this week is to make a list of what you need to make
the growth you want in your life.

- *Step one.* If you need more time, how will you make that happen?
- *Step two.* If you need money, make a plan to get it. A second job?
  A cut in expenses?
- *Step three.* Everyone needs support. Call or text or email two
  people and ask for their support. Be specific!

Unless you try to do something beyond what you have
already mastered, you will never grow. (Ronald Osborn)

To your transformation!

GROWTH #2

Self-growth *does not always mean that we've changed. It
means that we've stopped listening to what others say we
"ought" to be doing and finally live our lives according to
our own values.*
—Anthea Surokou, *Eventually Julie*

Sometimes growth is simple. It just means that we are growing into
ourselves and becoming confident about who we are as a person.

When we are young and live at home, we are subjected to the values of
our parents and guardians. We are also bombarded with the many different
lifestyles and values of the social network of people who we are exposed
to at schools and in our communities. From these early experiences, we
generally choose to live one of three ways.

First, we might emulate the lives and values that were demonstrated by
our parents because we find doing so safe and nonthreatening.

Second, we might discard everything that our parents valued as no good and fight to do the opposite, choosing a lifestyle from our community or social circle.

Third, we combine a mix of values from our parents and values of our own and create a life for ourselves.

We can change our lifestyle and values at any time based on how we choose to live our lives. That's called growth!

> If we don't change, we don't grow. If we don't grow, we aren't really living. (Gail Sheehy)

To your transformation!

GROWTH #3

> *Those who improve with age embrace the power of personal growth and personal achievement and begin to replace youth with wisdom, innocence with understanding, and lack of purpose with self-actualization.*
>
> —Bo Bennett

Life is filled with ups and downs. There are times when you think you're going nowhere or going in the wrong direction. There are times when you feel that your life lacks purpose.

During these downtimes, if you're open to growth and if you embrace the challenge, the only way out is *up*.

Nothing is guaranteed in life except change. And unless we change with it, we become stagnant and small. Our lives may become predictable and boring.

Some people start to believe that they are too old to change. They become fixed in their ways and in their patterns of living. They get comfortable and resist change even though they feel unhappy or depressed.

Change is uncomfortable! It's not easy. It's easier to stay home, under the covers and hide.

One can choose to go back toward safety or forward toward growth. Growth must be chosen again and again; fear must be overcome again and again. (Abraham Maslow)

Growth takes learning—learning about yourself and/or learning something new, toward a new career or new hobby or a new you.

There are many avenues for growth and learning:

- *Read, read, read* everything you can get your hands on about the topic that interests you.
- Sign up for a class.
- Talk to people.
- Volunteer to help others.
- Create a plan to take action so you aren't just thinking about it!
- Give yourself deadlines for action and stick to them.
- Get support—share your plan.

No one is in control of your happiness but you: therefore, you have the power to change anything about yourself or your life that you want to change. (Barbara DeAngelis)

To your growth and to your transformation!

CHAPTER 37

HAPPINESS

> Happiness is *when what you think, what you say, and* what you do *are in harmony.*
>
> —Mahatma Gandhi

It seems to me that everyone is often in search of happiness.

It also seems to me that many people seem to think that happiness is like an elusive butterfly—difficult to find, more difficult to catch, and impossible to hold onto.

Happiness as defined by men greater than myself:

- Happiness, according to Socrates, comes from knowing your deepest soul, your inner self, not from physical or external conditions. (The question here is, how do I know my inner soul?)
- Plato preached that man follow a moral code of behavior, living a life of wisdom, courage, moderation, and justice. These four pillars of a virtuous lifestyle would ultimately be the design for happiness, a pure and free life uncontaminated by worldly goods. (Give up my money? My car? Hmmmm, that doesn't sound feasible to me.)

- Aristotle explained happiness not as a state but as *an activity*. So, by *living our life to the fullest*, we are bound to become happy regardless of our circumstances.

So, it comes down to this—and it's pretty simple if you think about it in a basic way. How to be happy? (*And* this is your challenge this week!)

Live your life to the fullest! Life is an activity, not a spectator sport. Stop watching from the sidelines and start playing the game! Ask yourself what you want *to do* to be happy and go do it.

Of course, be mindful of the rights of others. *Act responsibly*, but have fun and be happy!

> You will never be happy if you continue to search for what happiness consists of. You will never live if you are (just) looking for the meaning of life. (Albert Camus)

To your transformation!

HAPPINESS #2

> *It isn't what you have or who you are or where you are or what you are doing that makes you happy or unhappy. It is what you think about it.*
> —Dale Carnegie, *How to Win Friends and Influence People*

Sometimes you might wake up and just feel "unhappy." You start saying to yourself, *I just feel sad. I feel like crying.*

You may start asking yourself questions, like, What's wrong with me? How did I end up here? How can I be so unhappy? There must be more to life.

Well here's the truth. Everyone doesn't necessarily wake up feeling happy and joyful every day. Some days are a struggle. It's a struggle to get out of bed. It may be a struggle to want to get dressed or to want to go to work.

Guess what? That's normal! *And* this is where/when your challenge really *is* a challenge to change your thinking and change your action.

Because that is how you will find your happiness!

When you are feeling blue, think about it, let it be, accept it for what it is, and set it aside.

Find something to be grateful for. It can be something small, like:

> waking up
> seeing the sun
> being alive
> breathing fresh air
> your dog's greeting in the morning
> a hot cup of tea or coffee

Whatever it might be, find something to be grateful for. It helps to change your thinking.

Then as you get dressed or get ready for the day, focus on the things that you can be grateful for and start to look forward to those things.

If you don't think that anything "good" is going to happen today, then it is your job—no, *your mission*—to make something good happen, even if you have to be a little crazy to make good and fun things happen.

Be a little silly if you have to in order to create fun.

> Sanity and happiness are an impossible combination.
> (Mark Twain)

Remember it is your thoughts and actions that create your happiness. So, get up and get out of your head, especially if your head is telling you to stay in bed and be sad.

> Happiness is not something ready-made. It comes from
> your own actions. (Dalai Lama XIV)

To your transformation!

HAPPINESS #3

> *Love is that condition in which the happiness of another*
> *person is essential to your own.*
> —Robert A. Heinlein, *Stranger in a Strange Land*

So now that we know what to do to create happiness for ourselves, what about creating happiness for those people who we love?

You might think that there is no such thing. I am sure you have heard the cliché that we are all responsible for our own happiness.

While the basis of that motto is essentially true, we can and, I believe, ought to look out for the welfare and, therefore, the happiness of the people we love.

If we are not trying to make the people, we love happy, then by default, we would be making them sad. And we certainly wouldn't want to add to the burdens in their lives.

You are one of the luckiest people in the world when you find some one person who loves you and some one person that you can love in return.

Your person may not be perfect. He or she may have faults or things about him or her that you aren't sure you can deal with over a long period of time. Your person may be older than you or younger than you. He or she may be fatter than you hoped or thinner. Perhaps your person doesn't like all of the same TV shows or maybe doesn't share the same political views. *But* this person thinks *you are fantastic*!

Your person understands your sense of humor! He or she laughs in all the right places. He or she helps you when you are overburdened and listens when you need a sympathetic ear. Your person is encouraging when you need a push and backs off when you need your space.

So, my guess is that your person is just about perfect for you!

Throw all caution to the wind and jump *all in* because your person is all about making *you* happy and you should be all about making him or her happy too.

> Of all forms of caution, caution in love is perhaps the most
> fatal to true happiness. (Bertrand Russell, *The Conquest*
> *of Happiness*)

To your transformation!

CHAPTER 38

HONESTY

HONESTY #1

Honesty is the best policy.

—Aesop ca 620–560 BC

Being honest is the foundation to all solid relationships. Although I am sure that not everyone believes this to be true—as evidenced by phrases like "nice guys finish last" and "only the good die young and so on—it is.

Some people believe that you have to be ruthless and dishonest to succeed in life, especially to succeed in business. They believe that the only way to get ahead is to walk on the backs of other people.

However, when you lie and create a dishonest atmosphere, more lies and dishonesty breed and grow, which creates chaos and upheaval. So, while there may be temporary success, there will not be harmony and success in the long run.

> Honesty and integrity are by far the most important assets
> of an entrepreneur. (Zig Ziglar)

Dishonesty in the workplace includes employee theft; submitting incorrect time sheets; lying to managers and coworkers; and unethical conduct such as theft, harassment, or drug abuse. When a small business experiences dishonesty in the workplace, it can result in lost revenue, low productivity, and depressed morale.

The Greek philosopher, Aristotle, noted that we are what we habitually do. If we practice being honest, then we will be honest and build honesty into part of our character.

Your challenge this week is to practice being honest in all areas of your life—which is not an easy task. There is fear attached to being honest. There is a level of anxiety that comes with being truthful. Face your fear!

First, be honest with yourself.

Second, be honest with others.

To your transformation!

> *Confidence thrives on honesty, on honor, on the sacredness of obligations, on faithful protection and on unselfish performance. Without them it cannot live.*
> —Franklin D. Roosevelt

HONESTY #2

> *The foundation stones for a balanced success are honesty, character, integrity, faith, love and loyalty.*
> —Zig Ziglar

Everything and everyone need a solid foundation on which to set in order to stand firmly during storms and to remain upright during the difficult times in life.

We establish our foundation based on how we are raised and on our experiences.

So, part of our foundation comes from the values we choose from our parents and the environment in which we grew up. The other part comes from what we choose for ourselves as adults based on the experiences that we have in life.

We don't have to like what we were taught as children or the things we were exposed to when we were young. We discard what we dislike, and as adults, we make our own choices.

This is when honesty with ourselves comes into play, and we establish our own solid foundations.

When we are honest with ourselves, we can say, "I like this or that about myself, so I think I will keep this trait." We continue to form our character based on what makes and keeps us happy.

This "look" at our behavior, our character, and our life takes introspection and possible change.

I use the word *possible* because there is no rule that says you must make a change. You don't have to change if you don't want to.

Being honest with yourself is simply looking at yourself and accepting that you are a certain way, which is important for self-love. Being honest with yourself is also important for change if you want to be different.

Practice being honest with yourself by keeping a journal or having conversations with yourself. But do *not* overanalyze!

Be positive and look for the good.

Be compassionate with yourself

Be forgiving *and* be loving

To your transformation!

HONESTY #3

> *Honesty starts with being ourselves, authentic and true to who we are and what we believe in, and that may not always be popular, but it will always let you follow your dreams and your heart.*
>
> —Tabatha Coffey

It may not always be easy to be honest.

Being honest with others and honest with ourselves sometimes means that we have to speak up. Sometimes it means that staying silent is the correct course of action. Silence can be honest too.

Speaking up without being hurtful is important. Sincere, kind, gentle, and loving words are communicative and honest.

Mean and vindictive words are not honest, even though you might think they are at the time. Those types of communications, while they may verbalize your emotions, are usually hurtful and do not generally convey the message you hope to get across.

Being honest often means being uncomfortable and going out of our way to do what is "right" instead of what is easy.

That sometimes means being honest with yourself and staying silent long enough to process emotions, which are temporary, in order to communicate effectively at a later time.

Honesty is important. It is important to know why you reacted emotionally in the way you did. What triggered your anger, sadness, or distress? Try to understand yourself before you communicate.

Your understanding of yourself will help you to communicate more clearly when you are ready.

To your transformation!

> *Treat those who are good with goodness, and also treat those who are not good with goodness. Thus, goodness is attained. Be honest to those who are honest, and be also honest to those who are not honest. Thus, honesty is attained.*
>
> —Lao Tzu

CHAPTER 39

INTENTION

INTENTION #1

The best way to insure you achieve the greatest satisfaction out of life is to behave intentionally.

—Deborah Day, *Be Happy Now!*

To live with intention is to be present in the moment. It's being in the here and now, without worrying about what happened yesterday or what's going to happen tomorrow.

We are all, myself included, guilty of thinking about things that went wrong in the "last conversation" or on the "last date" or in the "last relationship."

We scold ourselves for not having done everything or something that we "should have done" yesterday or over the weekend.

We get caught up in the worry of the "what ifs" of the future. What if I mess up this new relationship? What if I make the same mistake? What if he or she doesn't like me or doesn't laugh when I make a joke?

Your challenge this week is to live intentionally—to live in this one moment, this one day at a time.

Go to work or start your day with intention. Be positive about your day. Look forward to what you will do today to make a difference *today*.

Take intentional action to make a difference in another person's life by offering kindness. Share a smile, a helping hand, or a kind gesture—all go a long way to make a difference in another person's life.

Be a better version of yourself today.

To your transformation!

> *When your intentions are pure, so too will be your success.*
> —Charles F. Glassman

INTENTION #2

> *It is more Important to be of pure* intention *than of perfect action.*
> —Ilyas Kassam

Staying in action is the key to intention for yourself and for those around you. As always, however, there are times that your actions may be misinterpreted. That's when communication is of the utmost importance *and* your intention comes to the foreground.

It's important to allow yourself to be vulnerable and to let people know your inner self in order for them to understand your true intentions. This I know is not always an easy thing to do. It's often a scary and frightening experience to allow yourself to be vulnerable. Our brains often tell us to be wary and warn us to be careful due to some past experiences of pain and hurt.

However, to create a life of intention and to *be* in intention, we must leave the past behind us and stand in the present. Let the person or person(s) of *this* present day into our lives and express our intention.

When your intention comes from love, it is often received with love in return.

If you continue to have difficulty in this area, reach out for support. Call a family member or friend. Tell them that you are living in the past and need support to live in intention in today.

The longer it sits and the more you try to suppress it, the more it will turn into something bigger than it is (whatever the *it* is that's in your head).

Too often we go through life numbing ourselves of the present moment because we've for so long suppressed our true selves. Act with intention today.

To your transformation!

> *What one does is what counts. Not what one had the intention of doing.*
>
> —Pablo Picasso

INTENTION #3

> *Live with intention.*
> *Walk to the edge.*
> *Listen hard.*
> *Practice wellness.*
> *Play with abandon.*
> *Laugh.*
> *Choose with no regret.*
> *Appreciate your friends.*
> *Continue to learn.*
> *Do what you love.*
> *Live as if this is all there is.*
>
> —Mary Anne Radmacher

Be spontaneous.

Try and do new things. Love. Trust. Play outside your comfort zone. Live purely for the moment that is right now!

Aspire.

Your time is the most valuable resource you have. Choose wisely. Learn to say no. Focus on now. Commit purely. Listen to your heart. Feel good. Surround yourself with those who you want to become.

Commit to an intentional path. Discover the things that make you happy. Reevaluate. Reinvent. Grow.

The best is yet to come!

To your transformation!

CHAPTER 40

INTUITION

The intuitive *mind is where our genius resides.*

—A. Artemis

Intuition is the ability to know something based on how you immediately feel about it without research and without any facts. It is sometimes referred to as our "gut instinct," a hunch, a feeling.

Some of the best decisions have been made by intuition rather than through research. It's not that all research is set aside, but intuitive sense is used in conjunction with all other knowledge.

Intuition will tell the thinking mind where to look next. (Jonas Salk)

Successful entrepreneurs who trust their instincts and rely on their intuition have certain habits that we can practice.

Your challenge this week is to practice intuitive habits.

Successful people *listen* to their first reaction to every situation and practice intuitive habits. Listen to your own feelings and your own gut reactions to things. It is your journey and your experience so; you need to listen to and trust your intuition.

People who are successful are *mindful.* They are in the moment and are aware of what is going on around them.

They *meditate.* Meditation creates a peaceful and more centered you in order for you to be in touch with your feelings.

They are *empathic*. When you are in touch with other people and what other people are experiencing, it's easier to have gut feelings about what is going on around you.

They pay attention to their *dreams*. Your dreams can sometimes give clues as to what you feel or what you need in your life.

They nourish their *creativity*. Your creativity allows you to express whatever you are holding inside—inventions perhaps.

They *trust* themselves. Trust your feelings and hunches. You know best. Other people are not on *your* journey. This is *your* life.

To your transformation!

> *When you are confused about something, look inward, intuition is always there to guide you, let your feelings guide you toward what is good. If you feel off about something most often it's not something you should do.*
>
> —Jitu Das

INTUITION #2

> *Have the courage to follow your heart and* intuition. *They somehow already know what you truly want to become. Everything else is secondary.*
>
> —Steve Jobs

If you are having trouble making decisions, think about getting in touch with yourself.

That may sound ridiculous at first. It may sound silly or easy or stupid.

But take a minute or two to think about a decision that you are pondering. It could be something as simple as:

- Should I cut my hair?
- Should I get the blue one or the red one? (shirt, dress, car, whatever)
- Should I change my diet?

It could be something more complex, such as:

- Should I take the job transfer?
- Should I quit my job?
- Should I look for a new house or apartment?
- Should I stay or should I go?

If you take a moment and really become present to yourself and your feelings, you will find the answer(s) that you seek.

To your transformation!

> *If prayer is you talking to God, then* intuition *is God talking to you.*
>
> —Wayne Dyer

INTUITION #3

> Intuition *is a spiritual faculty and does not explain, but simply points the way.*
>
> —Florence Scovel Shinn

It is your choice to follow your intuition or not to follow your intuition.

Sometimes we don't listen to our intuition because we don't really want to know what our intuition is telling us. We ignore our gut feelings because we want certain things to work out a specific way, and our gut is telling us something different than what we want.

Many men and women have been fooled into walking a path that was not their own because they wanted or needed to believe in something more or different than what they had in their lives.

> Think for yourself. Trust your own intuition. Another's mind isn't walking your journey, you are. (Scottie Waves)

Stop worrying about what other people might think and do what feels right for *you*. Stop making yourself sick with guilt and physical illness over your indecision.

Give yourself some time.

Surround yourself with love—whether that's alone in nature, with a basketful of puppies, with a roomful of people, or alone in a bubble bath with your thoughts.

The people who love you will support you in all of your decisions.

Breathe and trust yourself!

> Listen to your inner voice … for it is a deep and powerful source of wisdom, beauty and truth, ever flowing through you … Learn to trust it, trust your *intuition*, and in good time, answers to all you seek to know will come, and the path will open before you. (Caroline Joy Adams)

To your transformation!

CHAPTER 41

JOY

The only joy in the world is to begin.

—Cesare Paves

Life is filled with a series of moments. Some of those moments are happy, and some are not so great. Like the expression goes, shit happens. But it's how we choose to react that's important.

There is an automatic emotional response to external events that we have that we may not always be able to control. For example, when someone or something triggers our anger, our sadness, or our anxiety, the first reaction that we have is not a happy or joyful one.

Be comforted by the fact that your immediate reaction is normal.

However, the length of your immediate emotional reaction is your choice, and you have the ability to choose joy even in the most stressful and saddest situations.

This is your challenge—to choose *joy*!

We have the freedom of choice in all things. Hence our emotional reactions are something that we can choose.

When you are sad, smile even if you do not feel like smiling. The act of smiling tricks your body/brain into thinking that you are happy. Your brain releases happy chemicals that start to make you feel better, less sad.

Exercise when you don't feel like it. The act of exercising will release endorphins, feel-good chemicals in your body, which will make you feel happier.

Surround yourself with people you love or with people who love you. Love creates joy! The more support you feel, the better you will feel. If you lack family and friends, find a support group or therapy group.

We can choose to live in joy! (Joseph Campbell)

To your transformation!

JOY #2

Joy does not simply happen to us. We have to choose joy and keep choosing it every day.

—Henri Nouwen

What does it mean to be happy? To have joy?

Everyone is always looking for the next best thing.

When I have a lot of money, I will be happy.

When I am thin, I will be happy.

When I find love, I will be happy.

Unfortunately, it just doesn't work out that way, and generally it's often too late before we realize it.

We break up with the girlfriend because we wanted more, and then we realize that we had love and happiness. We still aren't happy or joyful.

We quit the job in search of a larger goal, and then we realize that we were happy there.

We strive to be thin only to discover that we aren't happy even though the scale registers ten pounds less.

I am not saying that you are "stuck" with things the way they are and should never change anything.

What I *am* saying is, in order to choose joy, be aware of and be grateful for all the small and simple things in your life every day.

Be mindful of everything you do. Appreciate the small things.

Find joy in every movement and every moment. Be mindful of

your breath. Be present in every task. Look for the happy part of every relationship. Find joy in your journey.

As you are grateful for the things that life gives you along your journey, as you celebrate the joy you have every day, you will miraculously see what changes you need to make in order to have more abundant joy in your life.

It will all become clear as you become more joyful, because who doesn't want more joy in his or her life? And your choices will be easier to make. You may want to make big life-changing decisions, or you might want to make small alterations.

> Find joy in everything you choose to do. Every job, relationship, home. It's your responsibility to love it, or change it. (Chuck Palahniuk)

To your transformation!

JOY #3

> *We are shaped by our thoughts; we become what we think. When the mind is pure, joy follows like a shadow that never leaves.*
> —Buddha

My new practices every day are morning meditation and listening to joyful music as soon as I wake up so that my mind is first clear and then full of joyful sound to start the new day.

One of the things I think we all tend to do is get filled with the worries and anxieties of what has to be accomplished for the day or the week ahead, which robs us of the joy of living in the moment.

We have many tools to help us avoid this trap—one of which is simply to make lists and keep a calendar of the things that need to be accomplished so that our minds can be free to meditate and enjoy the moments of life.

It is so important to take time to play. Remember when you were a child and the things that filled you with wonder and joy. Bring some of those things into your life as much as you can.

Play hide-and-seek with your kids or with your friends. Play board games. Play cards. Finger paint or make crafts or bake cookies together.

If you had fun with your friend or partner on the night that the lights went out because there were no distractions of TV, computer, and so on, light some candles and pretend that the lights are out. Turn everything off and play together.

Find joy in companionship.

There is joy in playfulness. Be creative.

A joyful life is made up of joyful moments gracefully strung together. (Brené Brown)

To your transformation!

CHAPTER 42

LETTING GO

LETTING GO #1

When I let go of what I am, I become what I might be. When I let go of what I have, I receive what I need.

—Lao Tzu

Before you can become that which you truly want to be or that which you are truly meant to be, you must first let go of the past and all of the beliefs that you are holding onto. You must clear your mind and clear your spirit in order to become an opening or a clearing to allow the gifts from the universe to come to you.

The stuff from your past that you hold onto is like trash or roadblocks that create obstacles or block the good stuff from actually reaching you.

Create a visual.

Imagine that every fight or argument is like a brick in a wall. When you have an argument and hold onto the belief of the other person being wrong, that brick goes up and creates part of your wall to a good relationship. Every argument creates another brick that you hold onto until the wall becomes so thick and unpassable that you are unable to have a good or decent relationship with that person. Sometimes it creates a wall or unpassable obstacle so big that you may be unable to have a relationship with anyone.

When you start to *let go*, that is when you can begin to accept relationships *and* love into your life.

It gets even better. When you fully let go, love and relationships will start to automatically appear in your life. They will become abundant.

Your challenge this week is to examine yourself; really look at what it is you're holding on to.

What can you let go of?

Look at all areas of your life. Where do you want abundance? Relationships? Money? Education? Fun?

Let go and make a clearing in your life to receive that which you are missing.

To your Transformation!

> *Abundance is a process of letting go; that which is empty can receive.*
> —Bryan H. McGill

LETTING GO #2

> *Have you ever struggled to find work or love, only to find them after you have given up? This is the paradox of letting go. Let go, in order to achieve. Letting go is God's law.*
> —Mary Manin Morrissey

Often, we get all caught up in the "have tos" of life. By that, I mean we stress ourselves out by thinking and saying, "I have to do this!" and, "I have to do that." "I have to get this completed by this day/date".

We work under deadlines and pressure. Some of it is self-imposed, and some of it is imposed by external job pressures. We work hard not to fail and hold ourselves to a level of success.

We search for the "right" career path, the "right" soul mate, the "right" place to live, the "right" school, and the "right" clothes to suit the "right" style. We don't want to make a mistake, and therefore, we often get bogged down and don't make a decision.

Sometimes we need to let go and just breathe. We need to reassess.

We must be willing to get rid of the life we've planned, so we can have the life that is waiting for us. (Joseph Campbell)

Go with the flow and don't overthink everything.

To your transformation!

LETTING GO #3

When I let go of what I am, I become what I might be.
—Lao Tzu

Allow yourself to be loving and open to all possibilities.

Letting go of the negative experiences and people in your life is essential to your happiness.

Be strong and adaptable.

Learn to say no. Check out the book *The Power of a Positive NO* by William Ury and create healthy boundaries in your life.

Ask Yourself:

1. How important will this seem to me in six months?
2. How important will this seem to me in two years?
3. Is there a more enjoyable and productive way I could be investing my time and energy right now?

If the answer to 3 is "yes" or the answers to 1 and 2 are "not much," it's time to let go.

Let go and let love into your life. Create happiness and bliss.

To your transformation!

In the end, just three things matter: How well we have lived. How well we have loved. How well we have learned to let go.
—Jack Kornfield

CHAPTER 43

LISTENING

LISTENING #1

> Listening *is a magnetic and strange thing, a creative force.*
> *The friends who* listen *to us are the ones we move toward.*
> *When we are* listened *to, it creates us, makes us unfold and*
> *expand.*
>
> —Karl A. Menninger

Think about your friends—the people you choose to be around and the people you seek out when you want to share a moment of trouble or a moment of joy.

Those are the people who *listen* to you! They give you their undivided attention when you speak. They are not looking at their phones; nor are they distracted by people who pass by. They look you in the eye. They smile or frown and comment in all the appropriate places. They ask questions about your concerns or interject in your story. They are "present" in their listening to you and what you have to say.

You feel their love through their listening.

Listening is important in all relationships because it reflects interest and respect from the listener. So, whether you are listening to a relative, a significant other, a colleague, or a friend, *be present* in your listening.

Your challenge this week is to *listen*, to be present and not be in your own head thinking about what you are going to say next in the conversation or thinking about the other person's outfit or how you might be late for dinner. Just listen to what that person is saying.

> When you really listen to another person from their point of view, and reflect back to them that understanding, it's like giving them emotional oxygen. (Stephen Covey)

Your *listening* may transform and improve your relationships.

To your transformation!

LISTENING #2

> *Each person has inside a basic decency and goodness. If he listens to it and acts on it, he is giving a great deal of what it is the world needs most. It is not complicated but it takes courage. It takes courage for a person to listen to his own goodness and act on it.*
> —Pablo Casals

Not only are we meant to listen to others, we are also meant to listen to the voice inside of ourselves—the voice that tells us right from wrong, the voice that tells us to reach out and lend a hand to help others.

So, it's simple really, listen to the voice inside your head that tells you the right thing to do and then take action and do it. Listen and Act.

Listen for the need in others. Do not wait for someone to *ask* for help because *very* often people are not comfortable with the asking.

Offer assistance to others as you hear their need. Reach out and lend a hand. Your assistance may be small—opening a door or carrying a package. Your assistance can be great—driving someone to an appointment or cooking a meal for someone in need.

Do whatever you can to act to help others. Listen for their need. By helping others, you will be helping yourself. Your acts of kindness will transform you.

To your transformation!

LISTENING #3

Listen to the wind, it talks. Listen to the silence it speaks.
Listen to your heart, it knows.

—Native American Proverb

While you are busy listening to others, remember to *stop* and take time to listen to yourself.

We all get caught up in the hustle and bustle of everyday life and forget to listen to ourselves.

We all have the little voice in our heads and our hearts that tells us what is right for *us*.

We often overlook or push aside that nagging little voice as an annoyance. However, it can be our best friend.

When we listen to our heart, we make choices that feel "right" for us. We live our life with passion and purpose.

Listen to your own voice, your own soul; too many people
listen to the noise of the world instead of themselves.
(Leon Brown)

To your transformation!

CHAPTER 44
LOVE UNEXPECTED

LOVE UNEXPECTED #1 (OR UNEXPECTED LOVE)

Love comes from the most unexpected places.
—Barbara Streisand

As the month of February comes to a close, I wouldn't feel comfortable writing about anything else but love.

It seems expected for most people to talk about and read about and be about love around February 14, Valentine's Day. However, love, in my opinion, is important every day, and we need to remember not only to have it on our minds but also to see it and express it to everyone in our lives.

We are generally so busy looking for love, we often don't see the love that's already all around us.

We often forget to be grateful for the people we do have in our lives. Our family and friends, coworkers, associates, and even acquaintances—all of these people contain love, even if it's not obvious.

Remember that everyone is dealing with something. Whether that something is big or small doesn't matter, because it is the person's ability to deal with it that counts. So have compassion for other people's journeys. If a person seems grouchy or sad, show love by offering a smile and a kind word. If someone appears stressed, offer encouragement or see if you can help out. Sometimes just listening to someone is an act of love.

It is within our daily possibilities to create love with the people with whom we come into contact. Most of us go to the same places on a regular basis, so chances are you will see some of the same people on a regular basis. The person who makes your coffee or takes your cleaning or bags your groceries or owns your favorite restaurant might turn into a friend.

Start by complimenting the people you see. You have a beautiful smile. Or compliment the sparkle of their eyes. Or compliment their outfit or their hair or anything that is striking about them.

Your challenge this week is to create as much love as you can by complimenting people everywhere you go. Let people know that you see them. You never know what it could lead to as time goes by and one compliment leads to more.

Allow yourself to be that unexpected place for love to blossom and grow.

> Love can be found in unexpected places. Sometimes we go out searching for what we think we want and we end up with what we're supposed to have. (Kate McGahan)

To your transformation!

LOVE UNEXPECTED #2

> *It's amazing how you can fall in love with a person you didn't even notice the first time you met them.*
> —Crystal Sawyer

Love. It doesn't just happen to you. You make a choice, conscious or not, to be in love. It's a process really.

We meet someone. There is attraction or interest. Perhaps we share a glance, a look. Perhaps we have a conversation.

Or maybe we think, *No I'm not interested*, but for some reason we continue to spend time with this particular person. Something in the back of your mind or heart kept you interested.

We choose to pursue further conversation or ask further questions to see if there is mutual interest.

According to social psychology researcher Arthur Aron of the

Interpersonal Relationships Lab at Stony Brook University in New York, there are thirty-six questions that two people can ask / discuss with one another that will foster a close intimate relationship. After discussing these questions, couples almost always feel better about one another and want to continue their relationship. ("The Experimental Generation of Interpersonal Closeness" in *Personality and Social Psychology Bulletin*, 1997)

At the end of the set of thirty-six questions, you are instructed to gaze into your partner's eyes, in silence for no less than four long minutes, which is a closing and bonding experience for both people involved.

While I have not done this exact exercise, I have done others of a similar nature, and I will tell you that it is uncomfortable at first, filled with giggles, wiggles, and squirms. But it does conclude with a learning about yourself and other. You start out with the preconceived belief that the eyes are the window to the soul and end with something different. It is all within your own realm of experience.

Choose for yourself. I suggest for all to choose love.

To your transformation!

The best love story is when you fall in love with the most unexpected person at the most unexpected time.
—Alfiya Shaliheen

LOVE UNEXPECTED #3

There is another interesting paradox here: by immersing ourselves in what we love, we find ourselves. We do not lose ourselves. One does not lose one's identity by falling in love.
—Lukas Foss

When you are in love with what you do for a living, you find that your days just fly by.

When you are engrossed in a hobby or a project that you love doing, you will notice that you feel happy and light.

The same is true of being in love with another person.

You never seem to have enough time to spend together, and when you are together, time goes by quickly and you look for more.

(Now this may not always be the case because you need to nurture your time for yourself too, especially when you are accustomed to being alone a lot and/or when you have children.)

But when you are with a person you love, the time you spend together is easy time. It passes without notice.

We fear being in love, thinking that we will lose a part of ourselves or lose our independence or individuality.

I think its change that we fear or the fear of the unknown.

Whether we change our career, our address, or our habits, any change creates a level of uncertainty, and anxiety comes with uncertainty.

We may get fearful that we are making a wrong change, a wrong decision.

This is when we need to get out of our heads and have trust in love. Love is about building trust and intimacy over the length of a relationship.

Trust in the love that you have for yourself to make good choices. Remember to choose one another every day. Say," I choose you today."

Trust in the love that you have for your partner and trust in the love that your partner has for you.

When you have doubts or uncertain thoughts, share them lovingly with your partner. Communication throughout your relationship in an open and honest format creates intimacy.

> Every true love and friendship are stories of unexpected transformation. If we are the same person before and after we loved, that means we haven't loved enough. (Elif Shafak)

To your transformation!

CHAPTER 45

LOYALTY

LOYALTY #1

Loyalty isn't grey. It's black and white. You're either loyal completely, or not loyal at all.

—Sharnay

Loyalty is one of those traits that most people look for in a friend; a partner; and, most often, in themselves.

In many ways, loyalty is similar to honesty, as it brings out our integrity, and it shows us who we are and what we truly want.

When we know who we are, we tend to be loyal to ourselves and to our innate character. We then tend to be loyal to the goals that will get us to those things that we have planned for in our lives.

However, sometimes we falter in our loyalty to ourselves and to others along the way to our goals. Perhaps we are in a relationship that isn't going the way we hoped, and we fear making a change. Or we are in a career that is less than satisfying. We know that we need to do something to change it, but we don't know what to do, and we feel stuck. We have fear of looking for ways to get "unstuck."

So instead of facing the change, we act out with a behavior that is disloyal because doing so is easier than changing and less frightening. We break our own rules of loyalty, in partnership, in relationship, in friendship, at work and with others in general due to fear of being honest.

We tell lies, we steal, we stay in relationships that no longer feel right for us, we may even have affairs. All disloyal behaviors because we are afraid of facing change. We get caught up in the "what-ifs" of our own making.

What if I were loyal and said how I was really feeling about my relationship? I might end up being alone forever!

What if I was loyal and my problem persisted forever? Ugh!

What if I did nothing and stayed loyal to my job and stayed unhappy in this career?

We are human and we make mistakes in life. I, for one, have made many. The thing about making mistakes is to make a point of learning from them and moving in a direction so that we don't repeat the same mistakes.

Your challenge this week is twofold. First, recognize your loyalty. Recognize where loyalty is important to you. Is loyalty important to you as a personal trait? Is loyalty important at work, in friendships, in your intimate relationship?

If you have not always been loyal, forgive yourself for past transgressions. Recognize that you have been on a journey of growth and development, and now you have an opportunity to be loyal in all areas of your life—especially in areas where perhaps you were not loyal before.

To your transformation!

LOYALTY #2

> *Many of the qualities that come so effortlessly to dogs—loyalty, devotion, selflessness, unflagging optimism, unqualified love—can be elusive to humans.*
>
> —John Grogan

What is loyalty exactly?

We don't have an exact definition because philosophers disagree on what can be an object of loyalty. They argue that loyalty is strictly interpersonal, and only another human being can be the object of loyalty, while others believe that you can have loyalty to a nation or to a group or a cause or a job and so on.

In essence, loyalty is unyielding devotion and faithfulness.

If you feel that you have faltered in your loyalties to a person or to an area of your life, do not be worried or unforgiving to yourself. Loyalty is a trait that can be taught, and therefore, it can be learned.

The best way to learn how to be loyal is through practice. If you are not sure how, watch a dog!

Dogs are excited to see you when you come home from work. They have what seems to be limitless supplies of exuberance for life. They bestow unconditional love on their protectors and friends.

So, practice these following ten loyalty traits:

- Be enthusiastic.
- Be happy to see others.
- Share your time with others.
- Go out of your way for others.
- Be respectful of others in person and in absence—do not gossip.
- Be supportive.
- Be truthful, not hurtful but sincere.
- Be there for others in good times and in bad.
- Always be communicative—silence is destructive because it leaves people guessing.
- Be loving and kind.

To your transformation!

LOYALTY #3

When Leaders throughout an organization take an active, genuine interest in the people they manage, when they invest real time to understand employees at a fundamental level, they create a climate for greater morale, loyalty, and, yes growth.

—Patrick Lencioni

All people have the potential to lead others, whether they do so at work, in their family, in their group of friends, in their social circle, with their sports team or are simply a role model for others by leading through example.

It comes down to setting an example of morals and values. When your values create happiness and purpose for yourself, they may also create a level to which others can aspire.

That does not mean that you will be perfect in your journey. However, keeping your integrity, admitting to and owning your mistakes, and making corrections make us all perfectly human.

> The foundation stones for a balanced success are honesty, character, integrity, faith, love and loyalty. (Zig Ziglar)

So, whether you are at the work place, in your family environment, among your social group, or wherever else, remember to practice the elements of what you value.

If loyalty is one of your values, you may just be the leader you have been looking for.

To your transformation!

> *Achievement of your happiness is the only moral purpose of your life, and that happiness, not pain or mindless self-indulgence, is the proof of your moral integrity, since it is the proof and the result of your* loyalty *to the achievement of your values.*
>
> —Ayn Rand

CHAPTER 46

MINDFULNESS

MINDFULNESS #1

Living 24 hours with mindfulness *is more worthwhile than living 100 years without it.*

—The Buddha

So many of us live day to day in the pursuit of keeping busy that we forget to be mindful. We forget to breathe and appreciate the moment-to-moment beauty of living in the present, living mindfully.

It isn't necessarily important to fill every moment of every day with something to do. The importance is in the appreciation of whatever it is you are doing in each and every wakeful moment—even if you are doing nothing!

Be aware of your surroundings! Be aware of every sound, every aroma, every sight, every sensation, every breath.

> *Mindfulness* is simply being aware of what is happening right now without wishing it were different; enjoying the pleasant without holding on when it changes (which it will); being with the unpleasant without fearing it will always be this way (which it won't). (James Baraz)

Your challenge this week is to slow down. Take a moment to consider yourself and your place in the world. Be mindful of your own being *and* your own breath.

Give yourself permission to do nothing for fifteen minutes and enjoy the presence of the world around you. See the world with new eyes. Enjoy what you are doing in each and every moment, however small.

To your transformation!

MINDFULNESS #2

> Mindfulness *is the aware, balanced acceptance of the present experience. It isn't more complicated than that. It is opening to or receiving the present moment, pleasant or unpleasant, just as it is, without either clinging to it or rejecting it.*
> —Sylvia Boorstein

Many of us are under the impression that we need to be meditating when we hear the word *mindfulness*. However, it doesn't mean that at all.

Mindfulness simply means being aware and being fully "in the present moment."

Being mindful allows you to know yourself.

The only thing that is real and honest about life is the present moment. You never know what is going to happen tomorrow or in the next hour for that matter. Therefore, it is important to be aware and present for what is happening now.

When the present moment is filled with joy and happiness, you will be able to experience it to the greatest extent when you are fully present to it.

When the present moment is filled with pain and despair, you can experience it fully. And it will pass all the quicker when you are present to it and allow the experience to occur, instead of trying to block it, knowing that it is temporary.

To be completely engaged in whatever is happening in your life is the secret to enjoying life.

To your transformation!

MINDFULNESS #3

> *Be* mindful. *Be grateful. Be positive. Be true. Be kind.*
> —Roy T. Bennett, *The Light in the Heart*

The most important way to be mindful is to be ever present to who we are and what we want and need from life and from the people in our lives.

We waste so much energy trying to cover up who we are when beneath every attitude is the want to be loved, and beneath every anger is a wound to be healed, and beneath every sadness is the fear that there will not be enough time.

When we hesitate in being direct, we unknowingly slip something on, some added layer of protection that keeps us from feeling the world. And often that thin covering is the beginning of a loneliness, which, if not put down, diminishes our chances of joy.

> It's like wearing gloves every time we touch something, and then, forgetting we chose to put them on, we complain that nothing feels quite real. Our challenge each day is not to get dressed to face the world but to un-glove ourselves so that the doorknob feels cold and the car handle feels wet and the kiss goodbye feels like the lips of another being, soft and unrepeatable. (Mark Nepo, *Book of Awakening*)

Be mindful of yourself and others. Be positive with yourself and others. Be truthful with yourself and others. Be kind to yourself and others.

To your transformation!

CHAPTER 47

MOMENTUM

MOMENTUM #1

It's very simple; just look at your life to see where you're heading. You're always in a momentum *of something.*

—Maria Erving

Today's quote can be misleading in that it doesn't imply that it's simple to move forward in a direction of happiness or even in a positive direction.

It just means that, no matter what may be going on in your life, in spite of everything that you may or may not be doing, *you are moving*—period! You are in *momentum*! You are moving in the direction of something, whether you like that direction or not, is not the point.

You wake up every day, and you take action in your life by going to work or not, by interacting with the people in your life or not, by going out or not. You make choices to do things that make you happy, or not.

Your actions put you in momentum. Your actions move you in a direction in your life.

Your challenge this week is to evaluate the direction of your life.

Prepare to change your actions, therefore changing momentum, to propel the force of your life in the direction of passion and happiness.

To your transformation!

Momentum *builds success.*
—Kassem, *Rise Up and Salute the Sun:*
The Writings of Suzy Kassem

MOMENTUM #2

At the beginning of each day: pause, think about and decide
on what you need to do that day to continue to move forward.
—Akiroq Brost

Taking the actions and creating the momentum to move forward each day is different for everyone.

Each person is in a different mind-set or a different place in his or her life, so no two person's lists for the day will look the same.

It is easier to have *momentum* when you have a routine and follow a schedule.

- Get up at the same time every day.
- Make your bed
- Exercise, go for a walk, or do some other physical activity (twenty minutes is all you need).
- Take a shower. Whether or not you leave the house, get dressed as if you will be going out—it makes you feel better.
- Make and eat a healthy breakfast
- Write down your list of things to do for the day. This is different for everyone. Items may include errands, chores, work outside the home, technology, writing, social plans, career goals, doctor's appointments, entertainment, and so on.
- Eat a healthy lunch.
- Communicate your love to your family and friends.
- Plan a healthy dinner.
- Kiss your significant other.
- Write a gratitude journal.
- Clean up your living space before you go to bed so you wake up to organization and not chaos.

Prioritize *your* to-do list to your liking.

To your *momentum*! *To your transformation!*

> *Success is not a destination, it's the journey, the lifestyle and the* momentum.
>
> —Akiroq Brost

MOMENTUM #3

> *Sometimes thinking too much can destroy your momentum.*
> —Tom Watson

When you allow yourself to start thinking that you cannot do something or that something is not possible, your momentum will be stopped.

Your thoughts of what is possible represent the goals that you have set for attaining your happiest life.

Our fears and self-doubt are our worst enemies. They thwart any possible success by derailing our self-confidence.

Continued action is our friend! It keeps us out of our head, out of our self-doubt and on a path toward our goals and keeps us moving with momentum toward the life that we love.

Throw your doubts to the side and stay in action!

> Belief in oneself is incredibly infectious. It generates *momentum*, the collective force of which far outweighs any kernel of self-doubt that may creep in. (Aimee Mullins)

To your transformation!

CHAPTER 48

MOTIVATION

In memory of all those who lost their lives on 9/11, 2001

> *Believe in yourself! Have faith in your abilities! Without a humble but reasonable confidence in your own powers you cannot be successful or happy.*
>
> —Norman Vincent Peale

It is difficult to be motivated to act every day. No matter who we are or what we do, we all need reminders to stay motivated.

We look around ourselves and see others and then compare ourselves. And often, if not always, we come up short in our comparison. But believe me when I say that, no matter who you are and no matter how accomplished you are in your field, you need replenishment of the soul and rejuvenation of the mind in order to continue to be motivated. Doctors, lawyers, CEOs, teachers, millionaires, and construction workers—we are all the same in the end. We all need to be refreshed! We all need to be motivated to move in a positive direction. Some of us require more motivation than others, but we all need it.

Our motivation comes from our why. Why do we want the things we strive for in life? What drives us forward? Is it the desire for freedom? Is it power? Does money buy us freedom? Does it purchase power? Do we want security? Does money grant security? If we want health, are we motivated to act in healthy ways? Are we motivated by passion and positivity? Is our action creating what we want in our life?

We all have the power to create success and happiness in our own lives. We just need to stay motivated and stay in action toward our goals.

Motivation can be found through speakers. We can be inspired to motivate by seeing other people take action or reading something motivational and by setting small goals and taking small action ourselves.

Your challenge is to do one or more of the aforementioned items and get motivated to act, this week and beyond.

To your transformation!

MOTIVATION #2

> *Start where you are. Use what you have. Do what you can.*
> —Arthur Ash

Since all of us experience a slump in motivation, it's important to start where you are and do not listen to your own negative self-talk. Allow yourself your "slump." Take baby steps to get back on track. Spend time rereading your goals, but do not berate yourself for being in inaction. Instead, praise yourself for the action that you have taken and praise yourself for the changes that you have made. Acknowledge yourself for the steps that you have taken toward change. Be a friend to yourself.

First love yourself, or FLY. If you have difficulty FLYing at first—enlist someone to help you out of your slump. Email me! Call a friend. Call your mom. Talk to someone, anyone who will help you to get back on track. It has to be someone who will listen without judgment and without fixing— someone who will just listen.

If the person doesn't know how to listen, tell them how. Tell them what you need. It's the only way to get what you need sometimes. It will help! (You will also be transforming someone else into a better listener.)

To your transformation!

MOTIVATION #3

Don't stop when you're tired. Stop *when you are* done.

—unknown author

So often, I hear the words, "I can't. I'm tired." Whether it's in regard to going somewhere or doing something, it doesn't really matter. I just feel like it's another one of those lame excuses for *not* doing or going due to lack of motivation in life. We have a limited amount of time in life to do things and to go places, and if we lie back idly, then we will simply be watching life pass us by.

Yet neither you nor I can force other people to do things. We cannot force other people into action.

I admire those people who do things independently—who travel alone and go to museums, theaters, dinner, sporting events, and other activities alone. These are the people who get things accomplished in life because these are the people who are not sitting idly by waiting for others to rearrange their schedules to accommodate them.

People who are courageous enough to do things alone are leaders. They can speak to people. They are not afraid to make mistakes. If they are afraid, they go and do things in spite of their fear. They can turn mistakes into adventures and adventures into positive learning experiences.

Be motivated!

Take a chance and do something alone and turn it into a positive experience.

Have an adventure.

If you are tired, see your physician and get checked out to make sure everything is all right. Take vitamins. Exercise. Get moving.

To your transformation!

MOTIVATION #4

Set goals that scare you and excite you at the same time!

Be excited about what you want to do. Think about the future. Think about your goals and stay focused.

Be grateful for the accomplishments that you have made thus far. Write them down. Remember the struggles that you have overcome. The diplomas you have received from educational institutions were not just handed to you. You had to work for them. You had to stay motivated to earn them. You earned your first job, your first promotion, and your first raise. How many pay raises have you earned since you started? Be proud of your accomplishments! Be grateful for how far you've come since you were in college or trade school or high school. Give thanks to your higher power. Have gratitude.

How did you get where you are today? How did you get all your stuff? You had to be motivated to come this far!

Now imagine yourself five years from now, ten years from now.

Where do you want to be? What do you want to have? Envision yourself there and get excited.

Set goals! Make a plan.

I don't really care for Matthew McConaughey, but he made important points in his Oscar acceptance speech a couple years ago—one of which is to be your own hero.

Be *your* own hero!

To your transformation!

MOTIVATION #5

> *Only I can change my life. No one can do it for me.*
> —Carol Burnett

With motivation, only I have the power to make change happen. Only I can change my life.

If I want to lose weight, only I can change my eating habits so that I lose the weight. If I want to get in shape, only I can exercise, and only I can make the plan to lead a healthy lifestyle. If I want a better job, only I can make a plan to get one. If I want to make more money, only I can develop a plan to lead to financial success. If I want to have more fun, only I can make a plan to have more playtime in my routine.

It all comes to down to me, myself, and I. I alone and no one else can *act* and make the changes that I need to make my life into my dream life.

My action can be measured in progress, not perfection. As long as I take action every day toward my goals, then I am accomplished.

Life is not perfect; it is a journey of adventures. And along the way, we are supposed to have fun. Have some fun every day while taking action on your goals. Fun can be simple! It can be meeting new people, walking in the sun, playing with children or dogs in the park, eating ice cream.

Whether or not you do these fun things alone or with others, always, always talk to the other people around you!

That is your challenge for the weekend! Stay motivated.

To your transformation!

CHAPTER 49

OPPORTUNITY

OPPORTUNITY #1

Happy New Year 2018!

First of all, I do **not** believe in New Year's resolutions! They are too stressful! We make them. We break them. Simple.

I **do** believe in new beginnings and opportunity because that's what each day brings us—a new day and with each new day is a new opportunity for success.

> Authenticity is everything! You have to wake up every day and look in the mirror, and you want to be proud of the person who's looking back at you. And you can only do that if you're being honest with yourself and being a person of high character. You have an *opportunity* every single day to write that story of your life. (Aaron Rodgers)

Your challenge: Take this *opportunity* to be your authentic self. Be **real** every day this week!

To your transformation!

OPPORTUNITY #2

> *Every day is a new opportunity. You can build on yesterday's*
> *success or put its failures behind and start over again. That's*
> *the way life is.*
>
> —Bob Feller

Today is a choice to move forward, move backward, or remain the same and stand in one place. You have control over your own destiny, even though the pressures and demands of life make it feel like your life is spinning out of control.

Stop! Breathe! Breathe again! Think!

Think about the things that make you happy.

Think about the people that make you happy.

Make a choice to have more of those happy things and people around you.

Keep walking on your journey toward success

Your challenge is to push through your doubts. Perseverance pays off in the long run.

Success and opportunity are waiting for you through your next action.

To your transformation!

OPPORTUNITY #3

> *I'm a big believer that your life is basically a sum of all*
> *the choices you make. The better your choices, the better*
> *opportunity to lead a happy life.*
>
> —Karen Salmansohn

Sometimes people get stuck in indecision. What to do? Which way to go? How to move forward?

You have power over your decisions. You have the power to determine how you want your one decision to change your life. Making one decision doesn't mean you have to stay in that one path or with that one person forever. If we don't like the course, we're on, we are able to make a different decision at any time which will change our path. We consistently have the power to make new decisions. Therefore, one choice or decision will not trap you into something that will connect you to that one path or one person or thing forever, unless you want it to.

Think about the things in life that you *care* about. What makes you happy? Make choices and decisions that are connected to making you feel happy.

If you find that you are not happy after you have made that choice or decision, adjust your choice. You can always change your decision and move in another direction.

Every day brings new opportunities for new choices. Just stick with what you care about, and you will find that the universe will put opportunities in front of you. It will be up to you to make whatever choices along the way to move toward happiness.

To your transformation!

CHAPTER 50

PARTNERSHIP

PARTNERSHIP #1

> *The best* partnerships *aren't dependent on a mere common goal but on a shared path of equality, desire, and no small amount of* passion.
>
> —*Sarah MacLean*

Loosely defined, a partnership of any kind is when two or more people who are in a relationship get together and "agree to cooperate in order to advance their mutual interests."

Lacking the basic components of equality and passion to reach or maintain the desired goal, whatever that may be, will result in broken partnerships or failure.

Some partnerships begin with the components in place but break down overtime as extremely important pieces of the partnership erode and fall away or get replaced by other elements over time.

A partnership is like a breathing organism and needs to be nurtured and fed. It has to be checked to make sure that it is still running properly with all its components and that all of its members feel fulfilled.

The first component of any partnership is its possibility. Members of the partnership are generally inspired and enlivened by this possibility.

For example, the possibility may be saving lives or feeding the hungry or curing the sick or housing the homeless. It may be creating happiness or fostering love. Making money could be a possibility if that is inspiring, though that's not generally the main inspiration. Yet sometimes it is a side benefit.

The second part of any partnership is the commitments that are made by the partners who are excited to be the foundation of this new and wonderful venture. This could be a business partnership or a personal partnership such as a marriage or civil union.

The commitments are the things that each person agrees to in the partnership. Those include love and honor in a marriage or civil union. Equality and respect for both business partners and marriage is important. Communication is imperative.

The partners must decide what is important to them for their business and union to work effectively. Each partner is 100 percent responsible for his or her part!

Last and still important are the common goals and tasks. These are the expectations or the roles and jobs to be performed by the partners in the union. It is best if these tasks are defined at the beginning of the partnership so that roles are understood. However, expectations and tasks do change over time as the needs of the partnership evolve.

Communication helps to keep the structure of your tasks on point toward your mutual goals.

This week your challenge is to examine and evaluate your partnerships at work and at home. Are they functioning as well as they should toward mutual goals? Are all partners getting their needs met?

To your transformation!

> Alliances and *partnerships* produce stability when they reflect realities and interests.
> —Stephen Kinzer

PARTNERSHIP #2

> *The universe wants you to find partnership (purpose/*
> *happiness/pleasure/love/peace) with whoever (boy/girl/both/*
> *many/yourself) you want in whatever way (emotionally/*
> *sexually/intellectually/spiritually) you want.*
>
> —B. T. Gottfred, *The Handsome*
> *Girl and Her Beautiful Boy*

Partnership is created for the purpose of being in unity with others—of working together toward a common goal.

You choose that partner. You choose that goal.

If you choose to partner with yourself to work toward a goal, that's fine. And you will find success as you follow the guidelines for partnership and follow your plan. It's just a little more difficult because you have only yourself to hold to accountability.

> No man is an island. No one is self-sufficient; everyone
> relies on others. (John Donne)

People are meant to be together in community and to work together in small groups or in pairs. So, partnerships are a natural phenomenon.

Whether you are looking for a love relationship or a new hobby like hiking or tennis it is absolutely human nature to seek partnership. Perhaps you want to join a church or have been thinking of joining a singing group. Maybe you would like to take a yoga class or start jogging in the park with a running club or sign up at local public library and join a book club. Whatever your intention finding someone else who's looking for the same thing is part of fulfilling your goal.

It is all about coming together with common interests, common goals, and similar values and forming partnership with others.

To your transformation!

> *Sharing certain important core values is one of the key factors*
> *that determine the chemistry of a relationship/partnership.*
>
> —Assegid Habtewold

PARTNERSHIP #3

For me, marriage should be about partnership. *How can you love someone you have to take care of like a child all the time? A wife is supposed to be a partner, and yes partners help each other when they need it, but they are supposed to be together because they* want to *in my book, not because one needs the other.*

—Lynsay Sands, *A Quick Bite*

When partners in a marriage value one another and value equality, they see each other as equals, treat each other with respect, consider each other's needs, and support one another. They give one another the freedom to grow as an individual and work together to grow as a couple/family. Equal partners agree on goals together and work as a team to achieve these goals. They communicate openly and regularly assess their progress toward their goals and change things to accommodate their needs as necessary.

Financial arrangements are set up at the beginning of the partnership. Three bank accounts are recommended—one for each partner's personal use and one joint account for the partnership. This arrangement allows individual financial freedom for each person in the marriage and joint financial decisions as well.

It should be determined / agreed upon in advance how much money each partner will contribute to the joint account monthly. This is usually a percentage of monthly income, which may change as income or job situations change or family patterns change.

All situations should be discussed in advance. For example, does one parent not contribute financially when children are born? Will that parent stay home with the children? Will that parent get a financial allowance? Weekly? Monthly? Will one parent work part-time when children are born? Will both parents work full time?

Child-rearing beliefs should also be discussed, as well as whether or not you would even like to have children. Child care and children are important topics.

Visiting relatives is sometimes an issue in marriages/relationships. How often is too often? Do you always have to go together?

Setting up expectations in the beginning of your marriage/relationship is good. If you do one thing in the beginning and then "change your ways" without communication, it sets up resentment.

Partners *do* go out of their comfort zone for their significant other. It's called "stretching" when we do something that we really don't want to do, but we do it because the other person wants to do it. That's called love.

However, there will be times when our partners will do one thing, and we will do something else. You go out with your friends, and he or she goes out with theirs. That's called individuality.

You may even have times that you will be home together doing separate things—happily spending time together, separately. For example, one person may like watching sports on TV, and the other person might like reading a horror story. That's being together but separate! It's encouraging one another to pursue your own interests.

Whatever you do, however it is arranged, it's your partnership!

> The great marriages are partnerships. It can't be a great marriage without being a partnership. (Helen Mirren)

To your transformation!

CHAPTER 51

PASSION

Passion. It lies in all of us. Sleeping ... waiting ... and though unwanted, unbidden, it will stir ... open its jaws and howl. It speaks to us ... guides us. Passion rules us all. And we obey. What other choice do we have? Passion is the source of our finest moments. The joy of love ... the clarity of hatred ... the ecstasy of grief. It hurts sometimes more than we can bear. If we could live without passion, maybe we'd know some kind of peace. But we would be hollow. Empty rooms, shuttered and dank. Without passion, we'd be truly dead.

—Joss Whedon

Someone once told me that I had no passion. It was many years ago. *But* to me that was probably the worst insult and most haunting thing that anyone could have ever said to me. Truly, to have no passion, would mean to be dead.

We have passion every day of our lives—every moment that we are alive. We have passion when we love, when we are angry, when we are sad. Our emotions create passion.

None of us lives a life without passion. It would be impossible.

Your challenge this week is to determine what it is that you are passionate about. What causes do you support? Who/What do you love?

How do you spend your free time? Answer those questions to help you discover your passions.

I am passionate about injustice. I am passionate about my family and their well-being. I am passionate about education. I am passionate about making a difference for others, even if it is just in a small way. I am passionate about being a strong female. I am passionate about love. I am passionate about health.

To your transformation!

PASSION #2

> *Enthusiasm can help you find the new doors, but it takes passion to open them. If you have a strong purpose in life, you don't have to be pushed. Your passion will drive you there.*
> —Roy T. Bennett, *The Light in the Heart*

We all know someone who bounces out of bed early in the morning to go to work with a smile on his or her face, happy to be alive, happy to get going every day, energized, and invigorated.

That person is excited to start his or her day, excited to see what he or she can accomplish, excited to see what new things are in store for him or her today.

That person has passion—passion for life, passion for his or her work!

If you have passion for success, then you will be a success. You will happily work hard. You will do what it takes and more to reach the pinnacle of your career.

If you have passion for what you do in your career—drawing, sewing, planting, digging ditches, building—you will do the best at whatever it is that you do for work and you will do it with joy.

You don't always have to make your passion your job or career though, if you don't want to work your passion. If you are passionate about painting, you can keep it as a hobby and go to work at something else if that is what makes you happy or what pays the bills. You have to keep a sense of balance.

But take a look at other people and see what they have or what they do that you like. What is it about their careers that you like better than your own? Would you be happy in that career? With those hours? With that paycheck? That location?

What would I love doing If I didn't have to get paid? If I had financial freedom, what would I do with my time? What could I read about for the next few years without getting bored?

Look into those topics for work and see if there is a possible career there.

> Choose a job you love, and you will never have to work a day in your life. (Confucius)

No matter what you do, it is very important to feel fulfilled and alive.

To your transformation!

> *I began to realize how important it was to be an enthusiast in life. He taught me that if you are interested in something, no matter what it is, go at it at full speed ahead. Embrace it with both arms, hug it, love it and above all become* passionate *about it. Lukewarm is no good. Hot is no good either. White hot and* passionate *is the only thing to be.*
> —Roald Dahl, *My Uncle Oswald*

PASSION #3

> *You've got this life and while you've got it, you'd better kiss like you only have one moment, try to hold someone's hand like you will never get another chance to, look into people's eyes like they're the last you'll ever see, watch someone sleeping like there's no time left, jump if you feel like jumping, run if you feel like running, play music in your head when there is none, and eat cake like it's the only one left in the world!*
> —C. Joy Bell

I am sure that you have all seen or heard the slogans "dance like no one is watching" or "sing like nobody's listening."

The point is—live life to the fullest *now* because someday may never come.

Live everyday with passion! You may not get a second chance.

> I would rather die of *passion* than of boredom. (Émile Zola, *The Ladies' Paradise*)

To your transformation!

CHAPTER 52

PATIENCE

PATIENCE #1

Have Patience with all things, but first of all with yourself.
(St. Francis de Sales)

When I first wrote this section on patience, I was writing a blog and it was a new adventure for me as I attempted to send information to all of my followers through technology. Therefore, the theme of patience seemed more than appropriate.

Working on anything new, especially in the field of technology, takes patience. It often doesn't go well or smoothly the first time around. There are errors in learning. There are mistakes to be made. However, learning new things can be an adventure, a journey into a new realm, a new beginning.

Celebrate the patience it takes to start and finish new tasks. Congratulate the patience shown by others as they take on new projects and try their best to complete tasks.

Your Challenge this week is to have patience with yourself. Notice when you are starting to lose your patience. Notice when you are starting to be in a hurry. Notice when you want yourself to be better at a task or when you want others to get out of your way or when you want something immediately.

Stop and notice your reaction.

Take a breath.
Count to ten
Practice patience.

Patience is a virtue often overlooked. Look for it, recognize it and praise it!

To your transformation!

PATIENCE #2

Life isn't always easy, which is probably an understatement. We try to keep an open mind and a positive outlook even when things aren't going our way. For example, when you apply for a job perhaps one hundred unanswered job applications go by and feelings of frustration come and go. Other negative feelings creep into your psyche, among them anger, sadness, and disgust. You try to shake them off with ideas of running away to some tropical island or thoughts like, *I didn't care anyway.*

However, these ideas aren't the answer, they don't really make you happy. At least you aren't sure if they will make you happy. So, you continue to wait—with all of your *patience.* You continue to try to make changes through the proper channels of employment. You persevere.

Then one day, after application number 152 and more patience and fortitude then you knew you had—a job interview leads to *the job*!

You are *amazing*! *See yourself in that job.*

You may not understand today or tomorrow, but eventually God will reveal why you went through everything you did. It takes patience.

In our journey in life, there are people and things that are available to assist us. Sometimes we are not ready to embrace them. It takes patience to know when you are ready to accept the people and things into your life that can make great change.

Patience is bitter, but its fruit is sweet. (Jean-Jacques Rousseau)

To your transformation!

PATIENCE #3

It's difficult to wait! This is true whether you are waiting in line in the store, at the gas station, at the ticket counter, or at a doctor's office. You might be driving home from work after a long, hard day, and you're stuck in bumper-to-bumper traffic, going nowhere and waiting. It's frustrating. It takes patience!

Remember that you are where you are supposed to be when you are waiting—that there is a plan greater than you. Keep in mind the people who were late for the plane, missed their flight, and then heard later that their intended flight crashed. Had they been on it, they would have lost their lives. So, I repeat—you are where you are supposed to be at all times. It helps!

When you see other people, who are losing their patience, smile and, if possible, start a conversation or thank them for their patience. Everyone likes to be reminded that they are not alone in their frustration while waiting. You can start by saying, "It's hard to wait, isn't it?" or, "Is waiting easier for you? It's hard for me!"

These brief conversations help relieve stress for both people and might start new friendships. Hey you never know!

Managers who have patience with their employees show grace and kindness. Employees make mistakes without meaning to, especially when there are new programs in place. When managers accept the employees' errors in stride, give instruction, and have patience, it comes across as kindness and grace and is appreciated. That kind of patience is a motivator for an employee to try harder to do better. Patience is many things!

Patience is not simply the ability to wait-it's how we behave while we're waiting. (Joyce Meyer)

To your transformation!

PATIENCE #4

Nothing worthwhile comes easily or quickly, which is why *patience* is so important. The key, though, is to have a good time while you are working your way toward getting what you want.

Enjoy the journey!

People may look at you a little askance when you say to them, "You seem to be enjoying your journey!" They may think that you are weird, but there is fun in that game. Play with people. Have fun along the way.

> Happiness cannot be traveled to, owned, earned, worn or consumed. Happiness is the spiritual experience of living every minute with love, grace, and gratitude. (Denis Waitley)

Have the patience to live in the moment and enjoy the experience of every moment of every day. Do you know the practice of living in mindfulness? When you practice meditation and mindfulness, it becomes easier to be patient.

To your continued transformation!

PATIENCE #5

Endurance is patience concentrated. (Thomas Carlyle)

Patience is such an all-consuming virtue and can be used in so many circumstances. Life is not easy! If anyone ever tries to tell you otherwise, they're lying—or they are just trying to make life sound like it's fun.

On a positive note, life is great. It has its struggles and its ups and downs, but overall it certainly beats the alternative.

However, it takes patience to live a great life!

I used to get annoyed when I was in conversation with new people. They always asked what I did for a living. Back in the day I was a teacher of students with special needs. And always, always the response would be, "Wow, you must have a lot of patience!"

My reaction of annoyance was because I felt that I was undervalued. There was never a response like, "Wow, you must be smart," or, "Wow, you must have gone to school for a long time." Nothing like that was ever said. I was just recognized for my patience.

But patience is important for so many reasons. In a crisis, patience is important so you do not feed into the chaos of the current situation. As a teacher, patience is important in order to deal effectively with a diverse set of situations that pop up during each and every day. No two days are ever alike. No two children or families are ever alike. And it's important to be patient when dealing with them all.

Retail workers deal with a plethora of different situations and a multitude of customers during the day. Patience is necessary throughout each and every day because people can be demanding and often unkind. Yet the workers keep a smile on their faces, say yes sir or ma'am, and make it through the day.

When things don't go as you planned, it's so easy to revert to curse words, angry statements, or gestures. Remember to breathe! Thank everyone you know for their patience. Thank yourself for working on your own patience.

Forgive yourself when you have moments of impatience—after all, we are human, and we slip up.

Strive to be patient and be grateful when you are enjoying your patient moments in mindfulness.

To your continued transformation!

CHAPTER 53

PERFECTION

PERFECTION #1

Being happy doesn't mean everything's perfect. It means you've decided to see beyond the imperfections!

—Helen Keller

I remember when I was newly married thinking that I wanted to be the "perfect" wife.

I wanted to "do it all." I'd go to work, where I would perform excellently, keep a clean and lovely home, prepare delicious meals, and look beautiful all the time to attract my husband and keep it interesting in the bedroom.

My attempts to be perfect made me completely stressed out and miserably unhappy. I couldn't meet my own expectations because I was being a perfectionist and unrealistic.

First, I couldn't be perfect. Second, it wasn't possible to "do it all "— never mind doing it all perfectly.

After a year of futility and many nights of tears shed over my failure as a wife, I came to the realization that doing it all meant letting some things go—like dusting or vacuuming less frequently and getting it done *imperfectly*. And *that* was perfect.

I found satisfaction and happiness with myself and all my roles—wife, homemaker, employee, chef, and lover.

Embrace being perfectly imperfect. Learn from your mistakes and forgive yourself, you'll be happier. (Roy Bennett)

Your challenge this week is to look beyond trying to be perfect in everything you do. Which areas can you accept yourself as imperfect?

When you strive for excellence, you improve. When you strive for perfection, you will fail.

To your transformation!

If you wait for perfect *conditions, you will never get anything done.*
—Ecclesiastes 11:4, The Living Bible, 1971

PERFECTION #2

Find the perfection in every moment instead of trying to make every moment perfect.

Donnalynn Civello

As we head into this holiday season—Thanksgiving was two weeks away when I originally wrote this chapter—many of us start to feel the stress of making things "perfect" for our families and friends.

We strive to:

- prepare the perfect meal,
- set the perfect table,
- make the perfect centerpiece,
- create the perfect mood,
- give the perfect gifts, and on and on.

Personally, I've had Thanksgiving meals at my home so many times that I have lost count, and I think I get less stressed each year. But I still have some level of anxiety because I want everyone to enjoy the day.

So many things have gone wrong over the years. One year, the turkey didn't cook because the oven broke down. The cooking time was so much longer than expected that we ate dinner at 6:00 or 7:00 p.m. instead of the promised 3:00. On another occasion, someone turned off the oven inadvertently and the turkey stopped cooking altogether. The dinner time got pushed back once again. As a ritual, the dinner rolls almost always get burned, because I forget them at the last minute.

Oh, and I make terrible mashed potatoes every time. So last year, I tried a new recipe. The heavens were shaken and chaos ensued. I combined both sweet and white potatoes for sweet potato casserole, which was delicious. But I could tell by the confused look on the faces of my guests that they were lamenting the loss of their lumpy, mashed whites and candied yams.

We make it all so important. But in the end, nothing matters. What is important is that the day is spent with family and friends—with people you care about and who care about you. Everyone lends a hand, talks, has some laughs, and tells a few jokes.

I make a point to laugh at myself, my cooking, and all my attempts to make it perfect because it never is, which is perfect.

To your transformation!

This year I am thankful that I am not perfect and that my family will celebrate with me no matter what time it is. I did get a new oven though, so maybe dinner will be on time this year—four o'clock? — (if nobody turns it off, lol).

PERFECTION #3

Perfectionism *is a self-destructive and addictive belief system that fuels this primary thought: If I look perfect, and do everything perfectly, I can avoid or minimize the painful feelings of shame, judgment, and blame.*
(Brené Brown, *The Gifts of Imperfection: Let Go of Who You Think You're Supposed to Be and Embrace Who You Are)*

Brené Brown said it best:

> We cultivate love when we allow our most vulnerable and powerful selves to be deeply seen and known, and when we honor the spiritual connection that grows from that offering with trust, respect, kindness, and affection.

Love is not something we give or get; it's something we nurture and grow, a connection that can only be cultivated between two people when it exists within each one of them. We can only love others as much as we love ourselves.

> Shame, blame, disrespect, betrayal, and the withholding of affection damage the roots from which love grows. Love can only survive these injuries if they are acknowledged, healed and rare. (Brené Brown)

> Healthy striving is self-focused: "How can I improve?" Perfectionism is other-focused: "What will they think?" (Brené Brown)

Be perfect by being yourself!

To your transformation!

CHAPTER 54

PERSEVERANCE

Never stop fighting until you arrive at your destined place—that is, the unique you. Have an aim in life, continuously acquire knowledge, work hard, and have perseverance to realize the great life.

—A. P. J. Abdul Kalam

What is perseverance? It is more than just working hard every day.

Perseverance is the hard work you do after you get tired of doing the hard work you already did. (Newt Gingrich)

How do you establish a pattern of perseverance in your own life in order to achieve the life of your dreams?

- You have to set a plan for yourself, a goal that you want to reach.
- It's important to set a *positive* attitude—an attitude that is unshakable.
- Then you have to create a plan of action, which contains attainable steps.
- Be *decisive*! As a leader, it will be important to make and keep to your decisions.
- Have integrity. Do what you say you will do. Be true to your word.

- *Stick to it*! Persevere through it all, even when others doubt you and your plan.
- Form a group of support (three or more people)!

Your challenge this week is to select an area of life in which you want to persevere and follow the above guideline!

> Remember, it isn't the dreamers who have good lives—it's the doers. Remember also what I call the three Ps of success: passion, planning, and perseverance. (Homer Hickam)

To your transformation!

PERSEVERANCE #2

> *Live the Life of Your Dreams*
> *When you start living the life of your dreams, there will always be obstacles, doubters, mistakes and setbacks along the way. But with hard work, perseverance and self-belief there is no limit to what you can achieve.*
> —Roy T. Bennett, *The Light in the Heart*

I'm sure you've heard that hard work gets you what you want in life or that success is built by hard work.

Well it's true! Combine working hard with self-confidence and consistent effort on a workable plan, and you are bound for glorious success in whatever path you choose.

It may take time, but success will be yours.

You may run into obstacles and get discouraged, *but*:

> It doesn't matter how many times you get knocked down. All that matters is you get up one more time than you were knocked down. (Roy T. Bennett)

Get up. Get going. Persevere!

To your transformation!

PERSEVERANCE #3

Life is not easy for any of us. But what of that? We must have perseverance *and above all confidence in ourselves. We* must *believe that we are gifted for something and that this thing must be attained.*

—Marie Curie

I can't lie. It's not easy to get back up when you've been knocked down— when you have failed, and you are down on your luck, and it seems like all is lost.

There are always people who say that it cannot be done—those who think you are crazy for trying to do it "your way." They think your ideas are not viable.

Do not listen to these naysayers!

Stand up straight and tall.

Be proud to be you. Believe in yourself. Have the courage of your convictions. Go for it.

> Ask yourself, what is it that you want in your life?
> What do you want for yourself?
> What do you want for others?
> Create what you want for yourself and others with your words.
> Then make a plan of actions you will take to make it happen.
> Take those actions!

You may slip up from time to time. That's okay. That's human. Just get *back in action.*

Persevere and work toward your goals. Make your dreams your reality!

To your transformation!

CHAPTER 55

POLITENESS

POLITENESS #1

She already told me that she doesn't have to be nice, so why do I? Because my mother raised me right.

—Sheryl J. Anderson

My daughter came home from school one day when she was very young and complained to me with her little girl moan. "Why do I have to be so nice? Nobody else is!"

I sat her down and gently explained that being polite and kind to everyone is what we do. It's who we are, and it's important to be respectful to everyone.

While I teach that politeness is being respectful and considerate of other people, it's important to know your boundaries too.

No one should allow themselves to be abused or walked on by others. Everyone needs to know when to say no and how to be responsibly assertive. You can be courteous to others while asserting yourself and your position even when you disagree.

There are many reasons why politeness is important in life, but one of them is that, if you're polite, you are more likely to achieve your objectives and get what you want.

I place a high moral value on the way people behave. I find it repellent to have a lot, and to behave with anything other than courtesy in the old sense of the word—politeness of the heart, a gentleness of the spirit. (Fran Lebowitz)

Your challenge this week is to exercise your politeness muscle. How courteous can you be to others?

Say please and thank you for everything you ask for and everything you receive.

How else can you be courteous?

To your transformation!

POLITENESS #2

Please *and* thank you ... *two polite phrases which are slowly disappearing from our vocabulary.*

—Anthony T. Hincks

I practice the art of politeness in my relationship with my husband every day, and he practices it with me.

Some people think we are a little over the top— "crazy" because we have been together for quite some time, but we continue to say please and thank you to one another for all the little things *every day.*

He thanks me for cooking him dinner—even if it's just hot dogs and beans, which it is on occasion. I thank him for helping clean up the dishes. He thanks me for doing the laundry. I thank him for making the bed. We thank each other for unexpected kisses or favors or chores or things that get done without asking or things that get done after asking because it was a help.

Do *not* expect your partner or spouse to read your mind. *Ask* for help and say please and thank you.

We ask one another if we can help the other in any way. How can I help you today? Do this especially when you notice that the other person is struggling that day. Try to be aware of what your partner needs, but if you can't tell, just ask. What do you need from me?

Please and thank you can be used in all settings. Try it at work. If you're the boss, try it on your employees. They will appreciate it. If you are the employee, use politeness with your boss and with your customers. All of your customers will want to come back because they will feel appreciated.

> Courtesy, it is also currency. It pays to be lovely to people.
> (Janna Cachola)

To your transformation!

POLITENESS #3

> *One of the things that hold together a human society is the existence of basic politeness among its members.*
> —Yair Lapid

Have you ever noticed how much better people get along with one another when they come together for a common purpose?

They greet one another with a smile. They shake one another's hand and ask sincerely, "How are you?" and actually wait for a response.

These groups of people are not only gathered for a purpose but are also generating common courtesy toward one another and engaged in general politeness. Their behavior bonds them more tightly together as a group united in one mission toward one goal.

Wouldn't it be wonderful if all of humankind were to behave in this manner?

Some people propose that those who have ambition do not care what others think about them and do not need to be polite—that politeness is for the poor and for those who finish last.

My belief is that lack of courtesy is lack of grace. It is only arrogance that allows people to believe they do not have to be courteous to others. In time, they may or may not find a more polite journey through life.

In the meantime, it's our calling to do what we can for who we can in our small way. So be polite! Be courteous. Choose your words. Choose your actions.

> Politeness is the art of choosing among your thoughts.
> (Madame de Stael)

To your transformation!

CHAPTER 56

PRESENCE

When you take your attention into the present moment, a certain alertness arises. You become more conscious of what's around you, but also, strangely, a sense of presence that is both within and without.

—Eckhart Tolle

Being present in any given moment or situation is the most precious gift you can give yourself or give to another person. So, there is a play on words that I often use when someone asks me what they can bring to my home as a gift, I say, "Your presence will be my present!"

However, presence is more than just being there. It involves being fully engaged in the environment. It means immersing yourself completely in the conversation; in the sounds, aromas, and sights; and in everything that is going on in the moments that surround you.

You are tuning in, paying attention, and focusing on what's happening around you. You are consciously and effectively interacting with each and every moment as it happens.

Your challenge this week is to *be present* in every situation. You will be more engaged and engaging. How does it feel to you to be more present?

To your transformation!

PRESENCE #2

> *Being solitary is being alone well: being alone luxuriously immersed in doings of your own choice, aware of the fullness of your own presence rather than of the absence of others, because solitude is an achievement.*
>
> —Alice Koller

Your gift to yourself is to learn how to appreciate yourself for who you are with all of your perfection and all of your imperfections.

While it is pleasurable to share moments with other people and relish the company of others, there is no greater pleasure than being able to enjoy the pleasure of being fully present for yourself and full of joy in the knowledge that you are complete in and of yourself.

Some of us have never spent any time alone. We are afraid to be alone. There is a stigma to the word *alone* that implies loneliness. However, when we take the time to breathe, tune into ourselves, become aware of who we are, and become present to our "being," we can actually find peace and self-acceptance.

It may not come to you quickly. It may take some time. That means time spent in quiet moments, alone—alone enjoying your own company, enjoying your strengths, and recognizing yourself and your thoughts and feeling and everything you are!

Just *be* with yourself. Be present.

Who you are cannot be defined through thinking or mental labels or definitions, because it's beyond that.

> It is the very sense of being, or presence, that is there when you become conscious of the present moment. In essence, you and what we call the present moment are, at the deepest level, one. (Eckhart Tolle)

To your transformation!

PRESENCE #3

Life is available only in the present moment.

—Thich Nhat Hanh

How many of us live in the past?

How many of us are thinking about what happened yesterday or the day before that?

We wonder how we are going to get over what took place last week, and we contemplate what we did "wrong" or how we could've done things differently.

Or we spend countless minutes or hours worrying about the future. What will tomorrow bring? What will happen? We create anxiety for ourselves and others.

Life is *now!* Life is *this moment.* Live in the present. Be present now.

Put away your phone and your computer and be there for yourself, for your friend, and for your spouse or lover. *Be* completely present, in the moment to moment of every day.

If you catch your attention wandering away from the present, bring yourself back. Be authentic. Tell the other person, "I'm sorry. You didn't have my complete attention, and I want to be completely present for you. Will you repeat what you said?"

When you love someone, the best thing you can offer is your presence.

How can you love if you are not there? (Thich Nhat Hanh)

To your transformation!

CHAPTER 57

REJUVENATION

REJUVENATION #1

Every living faith must have within itself the power of rejuvenation if it is to live.

—Mahatma Gandhi

So, too, in order to live, we must rejuvenate ourselves as if we were a living faith. We need to treat ourselves with reverence and respect, being aware of our limits and replenishing our resources.

We go to work or school or play, raise children, care for our sick and elderly, volunteer at shelters or hospitals or food banks. We drive cars and spend lengthy minutes and hours in traffic jams or take mass transit and deal with the stress of schedules or delayed buses and trains.

We may take time to exercise our muscles and go to the gym because we know it's healthy. But even that, while it's good for you, takes a toll on your body by using up your energy reserve.

Then things might start to go awry. You might wake up in a foul mood that you can't shake. You come down with a "cold" or another type of general "infection." Your body and/or mind are just telling you that you need a break. You need some type of *rejuvenation*!

Your challenge this week is to listen to your body and your mind. Choose a way to rejuvenate yourself:

- Take a nap—twenty minutes for a power nap.
- Meditate for ten minutes. The more you practice meditation, the less time it will take you to meditate.
- Go for a walk outside in the fresh air.
- Listen to music that rejuvenates your soul. (Music choice is different for everyone.)
- Meet a friend for a heart-to-heart chat or just for a hug (hugs are rejuvenating).
- Do twenty minutes of yoga. (YouTube some stretches.)
- Take a bath—with bubbles or oils.

To your transformation!

REJUVENATION #2

Health is not simply the absence of illness. Real health is the will to overcome every form of adversity and use even the worst of circumstances as a springboard for new growth and development. Simply put, the essence of health is the constant renewal and rejuvenation of life.

—Daisaku Ikeda

We come across problems every day—issues with which we have difficulty. Some of these challenges are monumental, and some are small and seem easier than others to overcome.

Struggling throughout life is simply a part of the journey. Challenges may come and go as circumstances change. Yet no one ever said it was going to be easy.

Overall and lasting health—physical, mental, and emotional health— relies on how you approach your challenges and how you ultimately cope with the stress that each challenge brings.

Most importantly try to keep a positive outlook no matter how difficult or stressful the situation.

Practice rejuvenation! Make a list of your favorite self-care practices and check them off regularly. These may include:

- Keep a journal.
- Get spa treatments—facials, massages, foot reflexology, and the like.
- Practice aroma therapy.
- Participate in yoga exercises.
- Pray or do meditation daily.
- Socialize with friends. Have a lunch or dinner date or simply meet for coffee or tea.
- Exercise.
- Do deep breathing exercises.
- Take a nap. And get eight hours of sleep.
- Drink lots of water.

If you need more help:

- Crisis text line—text CONNECT to 741741.
- Crisis call center—call 1-800-273-8255.

To your transformation!

REJUVENATION #3

> *When you begin to meditate on a regular basis, you will start to notice that thoughts and feelings that may have been building up inside of you are gently released and you reach the quiet place that was always there, waiting for you—the place of pure awareness. It is there that you will experience peace, healing, and true* rejuvenation.
>
> —Deepak Chopra

When you meditate, you learn to "let go." You breathe in the fresh, new air of life and breathe out the old, stale air of the past.

As you push out the old stale air and exhale your slow breath through your mouth, visualize all of your stress leaving your body with your old, stale air. Breathe slowly out as you count to ten.

Breathe in through your nose—new, clean, cool, refreshing, stress-free air that lifts your spirit and energizes your soul. Breathe in slowly counting to ten as you inhale.

Imagine a beautiful garden or meadow with lush green trees, a soft carpet of grass, a sparkling brook cascading over the many pebbles, and rocks piled high from the crush of winter's snow. Smell the crisp, clean air as you inhale.

Each breath that you take in fills your body with a new spring life. Each breath that you breathe out empties your body of any stress you may have left from whatever you might have been dealing with yesterday or today.

Do this exercise for ten minutes. On each breath, count to ten when you breathe in and count to ten when you breathe out.

To your transformation!

> *Sleep and meditation are key. Natural sleep for 8 hours will help remove toxins from the body, help consolidate memory, create order from chaos. Sleep activates good hormones that are associated with* rejuvenation *and slowing down the ageing process.*
>
> —Deepak Chopra

CHAPTER 58

RELATIONSHIP

RELATIONSHIP #1

The most powerful relationship you will ever have is the relationship with yourself.
— Steve Maraboli, *Life, the Truth, and Being Free*

Your challenge this week is to examine your relationships, first with yourself and then with others.

What is your relationship with yourself? Do you listen to that little voice in the back of your head that continually says, "I am not enough"? Do you doubt your ability to accomplish what you want to do? Do you think that you are unlovable?

The relationship that you have with yourself is of paramount importance to all the other relationships that you have with others. It is the template for all of your other relationships. If you do not value yourself, no one else will value you. You must love yourself before you love another. By accepting yourself and fully being what/who you are, your simple presence can make others happy.

Perhaps you do not know how to love and accept yourself. Start small to FLY (first love yourself) the following way:

- When you get up every day, greet yourself with a positive greeting in the mirror. (Example: Good Morning beautiful/handsome! You are so inspiring, powerful, energetic, awesome ….)
- Be accepting of your imperfections. They make you unique. Embrace them and your individuality.
- Remind yourself that you do not "need" another person to be complete. You are complete just the way you are—whole and perfect with all of your imperfections.
- Do not strive to be perfect. You are beautiful inside and out just the way you are—even messy.
- Smile as much as possible, even when you don't feel like smiling. It will make you feel better. And it will help others feel better too. Always think about helping others to feel better.
- Share your love with others as often and as much as possible by being helpful, kind, and generous of spirit.
- Eat healthy and move around often!

You yourself, as much as anybody in the entire universe, deserve your love and affection. (Buddha)

To your transformation!

RELATIONSHIP #2

Being deeply loved by someone gives you strength, while loving someone deeply gives you courage.

—Lao Tzu

All relationships contain love. It doesn't matter which two people are in the relationship; love is always a component.

Yet we seemed confused by love. What is it? How do we define it?

Love is simply *acceptance* of one another. It's accepting another person exactly as they are *and* exactly as they are not.

For some relationships, this acceptance comes naturally. Parent to child for example is often a natural state of acceptance one of the other, especially in the initial stages of introduction. This is not always but often the case.

We sometimes call this unconditional love or say, "I love you just the way you are or are not."

This is also the love we, as whole human beings, strive to have for ourselves.

There have been discussions, debates, arguments, and concerns over the centuries about the definition of love. Poets have written sonnets and epics about love. Theologians have argued its meaning based on spirituality. Scientists study the effect on the brain and the heart based on chemicals released by emotional response. But no one really puts into words a firm definition of love.

We say we love based on instinct, and that may be partially true. Yet we all also have a set of beliefs or values that we have established for ourselves. Our beliefs and values set our lifestyle. When we make choices for a life / love partner, we want him or her to have similar beliefs and values so that we can share a similar lifestyle.

When we start to get to know another person, love may or may not begin to grow. Great relationships are about appreciating similarities and respecting differences. We meet and make our choices about whether to become friends or not and whether to move a relationship to the next level of romance or to end a relationship altogether.

A strong relationship requires choosing to love each other, even in those moments when you struggle to like each other, which is why it's so important for lasting relationships to be founded in solid friendship, connection, and understanding of one another.

> A healthy friendship is one where you share your true feelings without fearing the end of the relationship. It's also one where you sometimes have to let things that bug you slide. The tough moments will make you wiser about yourself and each other. They will also make you stronger and closer as friends. (Rachel Simmons)

To your transformation!

RELATIONSHIP #3

Far too many people are looking for the right person, instead of trying to be the right person. —Gloria Steinem

In my experience a common theme among the people I meet is that they are looking for love or looking for a partner or looking for romance with the partner they have. Sometimes they are looking for a romantic connection with a new partner because they are dissatisfied with their present partner and feel disconnected.

Some of the complaints that I hear include: My partner doesn't understand me. My partner doesn't pay attention to me. I feel lonely and alone even when we are together.

What happens is one person blames the other for everything that has gone wrong in the relationship. He or she doesn't help around the house. He or she doesn't pull his or her weight with the responsibilities. One person builds resentment toward the other.

Expectations are not communicated. (see section on expectations) Resentments build. Anger is the common feeling. Each person is waiting for the other person to "fix" or change his or her part of the relationship, so the relationship continues to deteriorate.

You are 100 percent responsible for every one of your relationships—100 percent!

You *must* invest 100 percent of yourself into each and every one of your relationships if* you want them to work and work well. It takes time, effort, communication, and *love*—lots of love—to make your relationships work. It takes accepting your person or person(s) exactly as they are and exactly as they aren't. That does not mean that you need to stay in a relationship that is toxic for you or one that is abusive or hostile. It simply means that you are 100% responsible for the outcome of your relationship, whatever the outcome. You get to decide what the outcome will be.

Most relationships will never be "perfect." But we can make them work with love and communication *if* that is what we choose.

To your transformation and the transformation of your relationships!

---

* Notice the *if.* It is your choice!

CHAPTER 59

RESILIENCE

> Resilience *is all about being able to overcome the unexpected. Sustainability is about survival. The goal of resilience is to thrive.*
>
> —Jamais Cascio

People struggle in life and prove how resilient they are during times of strife. With stress and despair, people falter, fall, and fail. And they either stay down or fight to survive to make it to the next event in their lives.

We all have experienced our times of desperation or times when we thought that life was unfair or felt so low that we that we couldn't go on. Perhaps you are having one of those times right now.

Maybe you lost your job. Perhaps you have experienced the loss of someone you love. Perhaps you have received news of an illness, which is devastating. Natural disasters such as earthquakes, tornadoes, tsunamis, fires all destroy lives. Automobile crashes can be life changing.

Stress can also be overwhelming, with simpler everyday chores that pile up around you. Workload, moving, parenting, and managing staff or financial issues all can require resilience to overcome.

Life is forever putting obstacles in our paths, and we are asked to overcome them. We are asked to smile and carry on. We aren't just supposed to survive, however; we're also supposed to grow and develop into better human beings along the way.

It's not always easy to navigate the obstacles that fall in our path. Sometimes we stop and say, "No, I *can't* do this!"

It's important in those moments to recognize that you are just "stuck" temporarily—that you are momentarily frozen. Give yourself time to de-stress. Take a walk. Take time away from the issue at hand. Go for exercise. Get a massage—whatever you do to unwind and take a breather.

Then come back to it, fresh, with a new outlook. Ask for help from a friend or family member. Get support from a neighbor or from the community

Your challenge this week is to think about all of the obstacles that you have overcome so far in your life, big and small.

Make a list. How did you overcome these obstacles? Write down the methods that you have used in the past. Congratulate yourself for overcoming those obstacles!

To your transformation!

> *Do not judge me by my success, judge me by how many times I fell down and got back up again.*
> —Nelson Mandela

RESILIENCE #2

> Resilience *isn't a single skill. It's a variety of skills and coping mechanisms. To bounce back from bumps in the road as well as failures, you should focus on emphasizing the positive.*
> —Jean Chatzky

Build a support system (as mentioned earlier). Good relationships with close family members, friends, or others are important. Accepting help and support from those who care about you and will listen to you without judgment strengthens resilience. Assisting others in their time of need also can benefit you.

Try to avoid seeing your problem or difficulty as an insurmountable problem. You can't change the fact that highly stressful events happen, but you can change how you interpret and respond to these events.

Accept that change is a part of living. Certain goals that you had may no longer be attainable as a result of problems or situations that have occurred. Accepting the way things are now—your new normal—can help you focus on things that you *can* change.

Move toward your goals. Develop some realistic goals. Do something regularly—even if it seems like a small accomplishment—that enables you to move toward your goals. Make a daily action plan to accomplish at least *one* thing every day. Write it down and do it!

Ask yourself, "What's one thing I know I can accomplish today that helps me move in the direction I want to go?"

Look for ways to learn something new about yourself. People often learn something about themselves and may find that they have grown in some respect as a result of their struggle with loss. Many people who have experienced tragedies and hardship have reported better relationships, greater sense of strength even while feeling vulnerable, increased sense of self-worth, a more developed spirituality, and heightened appreciation for life.

Nurture a positive view of yourself. Developing confidence in your ability to solve problems and trusting your instincts helps build resilience.

Keep things in perspective. Even when facing very painful events, try to consider the stressful situation in a broader context and keep a long-term perspective. Avoid blowing the event out of proportion. Avoid words like *always* and *never*.

Maintain a hopeful outlook. An optimistic outlook enables you to expect that good things will happen in your life. Try visualizing what you want, rather than focusing on your fears.

Take care of yourself. Pay attention to your own needs and feelings. Engage in activities that you enjoy and find relaxing. Exercise regularly. Taking care of yourself helps to keep your mind and body prepared to deal with situations that require resilience.

Additional ways of strengthening resilience may be helpful. For example, some people write about (keep a journal of) their deepest thoughts and feelings related to trauma or other stressful events in their life. Meditation and spiritual practices help some people build connections and restore hope.

The key is to identify ways that are likely to work well for you as part of your own personal strategy for building resilience.

To your transformation!

RESILIENCE #3

> *My scars remind me that I did indeed survive my deepest wounds. That in itself is an accomplishment. And they bring to mind something else, too. They remind me that the damage life has inflicted on me has, in many places, left me stronger and more* resilient. *What hurt me in the past has actually made me better equipped to face the present.*
>
> —Steve Goodier

Being resilient isn't easy. It is born of emotional pain and, at times, physical burden. Through much difficulty, however, and after surviving whatever hardships are thrown our way, we seem to come out of trauma and pain stronger somehow. Lyricists write songs about how "what doesn't kill you makes you stronger."

To your strength and to your transformation!

> *Out of massive suffering emerged the strongest souls; the most massive character are seared with scars.*
>
> —Khalil Gibran

CHAPTER 60

RESPONSIBILITY

RESPONSIBILITY #1

Responsibility is a choice for who I am and what I do. It means that I take a stand for my choices! It means that I arrive on time and follow through with my promises. I am accountable for my actions and true to my word. When I say that I'm going to do something, I do it. I complete tasks even if I don't feel like it, especially if I have given my word that the task will be completed by a certain time. It is my responsibility to complete my task and keep my word. When I say that I'm going to be somewhere, I'm there—even if I don't feel like going when the time comes.

> You are always responsible for how you act, no matter how you Feel! (Robert Tew)

If someone asks me to keep a confidence, I keep it. Someone else's information is not mine to disclose to others.

Your challenge this week is to be aware of your responsibilities and step up to them with eagerness. List your responsibilities and check them off daily as you complete them. Be proud of your task completion!

Also recognize others who step up to their responsibilities and show your appreciation.

To your transformation!

RESPONSIBILITY #2

I am not only responsible for myself but I am also responsible for others. It is my global responsibility to reach out and help my neighbor, my fellow man or woman.

As I was driving home from my seminar tonight, I noticed a car broken down on the side of the parkway. There was a family sitting on the grassy hill with children. Mind you, I was driving at sixty-five miles per hour, and it was dark, so I only got a quick glance at the broken-down car and the family on the hill. I quickly glanced at the mile marker, which was 151.7, and took a mental note to myself that, if I was that family, I would want someone to help me.

About two or three miles ahead there happened to be a state police station, so I pulled off, went inside and reported the broken-down car and the family on the side of the road. The desk officer thanked me for the information and told me that they would look into the situation.

Now I don't know if the family was assisted after that but at least I felt like I did something to help.

It is our responsibility to find a way to safely help others in some way, no matter how small, even if it is indirectly.

By helping others, I win and they win. It's a win-win for both parties. (Win-win means both sides gain something positive in the outcome.)

I challenge you to not only be responsible for yourself but also for others. That can include your friends, your family, your coworkers, acquaintances, and/or strangers. Just reach out and assist someone. Your responsibility can transform others' lives as well as your own.

To your transformation!

RESPONSIBILITY #3

Responsibility to yourself means following through on your commitments to yourself. When you say you are going to do something for yourself, *do it*!

For example, let's say I tell myself I am going to lose five pounds. Then it never comes off. In fact, I/you gain five more in the interim. Or I say I'm going to start exercising. I might get excited for this plan and join a gym, go to the gym once or twice, and never go again. Then I feel terrible about myself and about my emptiness.

Millions of people make empty promises every year over and over again and again.

Responsibility to yourself means keeping your promises to yourself first. If you cannot keep a promise to yourself, how can you expect to keep a promise to another person?

If you say, I'm going to lose five pounds and follow through by taking action to do so—by rearranging the food supply in your house so that you cook healthy and, therefore, eat healthy—those five pounds are more likely to disappear over a designated period of time.

You might make an exercise plan that you can manage in your daily routine, one that you can stick to and do on a daily or semi-daily basis. Your exercise routine might include walking outside or a yoga routine that you found on YouTube or exercises that you listed on a piece of paper that you can complete in thirty minutes.

Thirty or even twenty minutes of exercise each day is better than zero exercise every day. You'll be on the road to a healthier you!

Make a list of the things that you want to accomplish and check off the tasks that you accomplish each day. Make a new list at the beginning of each new day. It gives you a sense of pride and completion when you can literally check things off your list every day.

Share your accomplishments with a friend or family member. Get support if you are struggling to complete your tasks and also get support when you complete those tasks so that you can celebrate together. Be proud.

To your transformation!

RESPONSIBILITY #4

Take responsibility for your mistakes past and present!

It's okay to make mistakes. It's why the eraser was invented. What a wonderful invention, the eraser. I love to use pencils and wish I could live my life in pencil, because I make lots of mistakes that I wish I could just erase. But alas, life doesn't work that simply.

I have made many mistakes in my life, some large, some small, some that I am still trying to make up for, some that have been forgiven, and some not yet forgiven. What I have learned, though, is that it's important to admit to and own your mistakes—to apologize, forgive yourself, and move on.

You can't undo what has been done. You can't take back your words. You can't take back your actions.

You can, however, make new possibilities for yourself and others with hope and promise by accepting your responsibility for your actions.

Be authentic, loving and genuine.

To your transformation!

RESPONSIBILITY #5

Make a difference in the world today and every day through your responsibility to yourself and others. Ask yourself a simple question: Am I happy with the state of the world? With the state of my community? With the state of my social circle? With the state of my family? Really happy?

What can you do to make it better? Simple things mean a lot!

Offer words of encouragement and praise. Talk to people. Walk through your neighborhood and get to know your neighbors. Ask, "How can I help you?" And then *step up*!

Smile at strangers. Open doors. Help someone carry packages. Let people go in front of you in line. Tell the cashier that he or she is doing a great job. Talk to everyone as equals. Ask people's name. Shake people's hand.

It doesn't take money to make a difference in the life of another human being. It just takes some of your time to be present in another person's life. In some cases, your small interaction could mean the difference between life and death. You never know what is going on for other people and what other people are dealing with—their struggles, their demons.

Be responsible today and every day. Share yourself with others! It only takes a minute and a smile. The power of your smile is priceless.

To your transformation!

CHAPTER 61

ROMANCE

ROMANCE #1

Vulnerability is the essence of romance. It's the art of being uncalculated. The willingness to look foolish, the courage to say, "This is me, and I'm interested in you enough to show you my flaws with the hope that you may embrace me for all that I am but, more important, all that I am not."
—Ashton Kutcher

Ah, romance—the ever elusive, ever desired rare gem of life!

We have a love affair with the "idea" of romance. And yet, we don't agree on what truly is romantic, because it's different for everyone.

Ask around:

Ah … romance to me is spontaneity. It's not diamond earrings; it's a bunch of daffodils that's freshly picked from the field. (Kate Winslet)

I think that romance sort of coincides with effort, so you can fall flat on your face, but as long as you're making a great effort, I think it comes off as romantic. So, it can be something as simple as, like, if you're someone who doesn't cook, you can make a meal. (Ashton Kutcher)

If a man lets all of my dogs sleep in the bed with us, then that is the most romantic thing. You must love my dogs in order to love me. A man who is nice to my animals and doesn't shoo them away—well, that's the height of romance. (Salma Hayek)

I think romance is anything honest. As long as it's honest, it's so disarming. (Kristen Stewart)

The definition of romance, according to *Webster*, is "a fictitious tale of wonderful and extraordinary events characterized by much imagination and idealization."

Romance is made up. It is make-believe. Romance is a way of being.

Your challenge this week is to determine your way of being romantic. Identify what is romantic to you. How do you want to include romance in your life? You can do romantic things with another person *and* with yourself.

To love oneself is the beginning of a lifelong romance. (Oscar Wilde)

Make a list of your romantic things to do. For example:

- Sip wine by candlelight and/or have dinner by candlelight.
- Buy yourself flowers.
- Go on an overnight trip.
- Have a luxury spa treatment.
- Give/get a foot massage
- Have a picnic.
- Go to the car show.
- See a concert.
- Take a hike in the forest.
- See the sunset/sunrise.

Be creative! Think out of the box.

Be romantic. What is romantic to me may not be romantic to you and vice versa.

To your transformation!

ROMANCE #2

> *I think it's wonderful when a love story begins with a great deal of romance and affection, passion and excitement, that's how it should be. But I don't necessarily know that it's the wisest thing in the world to expect that it ends there, or that it should, 30 years down the road, it should still look as it did on the night of your first kiss.*
>
> —Elizabeth Gilbert

We are *all* guilty of getting caught up in the idea that love is not romance and romance is not love.

In fact, the reverse is actually true. Love and romance are interchangeable. Love *is* romance, and romance *is* love.

And right about now, you are probably thinking that I am crazy!

However, here is my truth. We all get caught up in movies, books, and TV—media explosions of what society wants us to believe the true definition of Romance is. We take those media descriptions as biblical truths and hold on tight.

In fact, this is not *real* romance.

Romance is whatever *you* want it to be—period. So, whatever is or was romantic at the beginning of your relationship with either yourself or with another person is what can still be romantic now.

However, life does change and our circumstances change. Children are born. Jobs change. We move and have different demands on our time.

That doesn't mean we can't continue to be romantic while we love ourselves and/or someone else. It is all about what suits you or you and your partner best.

Wash the dishes, even though you cooked. Change the baby's diaper, when it's not your turn. Clean the house before he or she gets home. Or hire a cleaning service for yourself. Do chores together, even though you don't feel like it and even though he or she didn't ask you to help.

Hold hands. Kiss for no reason. Reach over and touch him or her. Be happy to see him or her when he or she gets home from work. Rush to greet him or her with a hug and smile. Give the other person space if that is what he or she crave.

Send a romantic text or email for no reason—thinking of you. Make a special cup of tea or coffee. Let him or her control the TV remote.

> Romance is thinking about your significant other, when you are supposed to be thinking about something else. (Nicholas Sparks)

To your Transformation!

ROMANCE #3

> *Romance is the glamour, which turns the dust of everyday life into a golden haze.*
> —Carolyn Gold Heilbrun

Romance does not have to be *only* between love partners. It can be between two people of any connection, or it can be found in a group of people who share a common appreciation.

Romance is a mythical and wondrous invention of our imagination. It is created by our senses, by what we find intoxicating and beautiful.

You can share a romantic experience of the baking of homemade cookies with a six-year-old, enjoying the texture of the dough, the sounds of the utensils, the aromas of the freshly baked foods, and the joy of spending time together.

Hiking in nature can be a romantic adventure shared with friends. Discovering hidden pathways through the woods, engaging in conversation, and sharing refreshments along your journey all can lead to better understandings and deeper relationships.

When you find a topic that you love to learn about and are eager to share with others, there is a certain romance to your sharing. You are exuberant about what you know and share with passion and energy.

All the great teachers of the world have fallen in love with their subject and found romance in the learning and sharing of their wisdom.

Mathematics has beauty and romance. It's not a boring place to be, the mathematical world. It's an extraordinary place; it's worth spending time there. (Marcus du Sautoy)

Science is not only a disciple of reason but, also, one of romance and passion. (Stephen Hawking)

Find your passion and share the romance.

Singing is my passion, my first love and the secret of my energy. Music to me is like finding my inner self, my soul. It gives me a great joy to see audiences enjoying with me. I have given my heart to singing. When I sing, I can feel *romance* in everything around me. (Kailash Kher)

To your transformation!

CHAPTER 62
SELF-ACTUALIZATION

SELF-ACTUALIZATION #1

What a man can be, he must be. This need we may call self-actualization ... *It refers to the desire for self-fulfillment, namely, to the tendency for him to become* actualized *in what he is potentially. This tendency might be phrased as the desire to become more and more what one is, to become everything that one is capable of becoming.*

—Abraham Maslow, *Motivation and Personality*, 1954, 93

How do we fulfill our potential? How do we become everything that we are meant to become?

Through action!

The word *act* is the first part of the word *actualization* by no accident. In order to become *self-actualized*, we all must take action.

Action is not a temporary state of being but a constant state of movement toward fulfillment.

Your challenge this week is to take action! Recognize what you want in life—what will make you happy and fulfilled. Make a list of actions that you can take toward those goals. Your actions can be small, medium, or big (the bigger the better, but you can start your actions where you are comfortable and move toward bigger actions.

Check your completed actions off your list. Yay *you*!

To your transformation!

> *I can feel guilty about the past, Apprehensive about the future, but only in the present can I act.*
>
> —Abraham Maslow

SELF-ACTUALIZATION #2

One can choose to go back toward safety or forward toward growth. Growth must be chosen again and again; fear must be overcome again and again.

Abraham Maslow's theory of self-actualization and personal growth can be frightening because it implies that you have to be in action all of the time, which is difficult due to the fear that we all must push aside in order to complete the tasks that we have assigned ourselves for our ultimate path in life.

Be in action as much as possible!

Do so even though you have fears.

Sometimes we want to stick our head in the proverbial sand and go back to our old habits and hide ourselves from the possibility of being the best possible person that we can become. It's easier and safer in the old, safe version of ourselves.

Yet, when we are able to overcome our fears (for example, speaking in public, going on a date, flying in a plane, riding a bike, applying for a new job, or whatever it may be), we feel a sense of accomplishment, strength, and renewal. We are energized by our achievement no matter how small, especially if we are able to share it with someone who is able to acknowledge it with us and recognize our feat.

If no one was there with you, make sure you share your accomplishment with a friend or a partner, someone who will share your joy and who will encourage you to continue to move toward growth and self-actualization.

Happiness shared is happiness doubled.

To your transformation!

SELF-ACTUALIZATION #3

A person who makes full use of and exploits his talents, potentialities, and capacities. Such a person seems to be fulfilling himself and doing the best he is capable of doing. The self-actualized person must find in his life those qualities that make his living rich and rewarding. He must find meaningfulness, self-sufficiency, effortlessness, playfulness, richness, simplicity, completion, necessity, perfection, individuality, beauty, and truth.

—Abraham Maslow

We all see them—those people we admire. The happy people! The beautiful people! The people for whom we have the slightest envy or the small thoughts that niggle at the back of our minds that say, *I want to be like him or her. I want what he or she has.*

Well, there's no secret to having what they have. They don't drink a magic potion or have special powers that you do not possess.

They simply use *everything* that they have. They are *in action* every day. They act the way that they want to be. They act the way they want to live! And the rest of their life follows.

So simple, you say. *It can never be*, you think. And those thoughts will hold you back from your own greatness.

Think of everything that you want and take action. Act as if you already are the person that has it all.

If you want love, act like you have it, and it will be yours.

If you want money, act like you have it, and it will be yours.

If you want health, act like you have it, and it will be yours.

If you want happiness, act happy, and you will be happy.

Your mind is powerful, and you can create whatever you want by your thoughts and your actions.

Think and *act* in the way you want to live your life.

To your transformation!

CHAPTER 63

SELF-LOVE

SELF-LOVE #1

If you have the ability to love, love yourself first.
—Charles Bukowski

Self-love does not seem to come naturally to many people. So, it is important to nurture yourself and your love for yourself in order to develop a healthy relationship with yourself.

Loving yourself starts with self-acceptance. Accept yourself for who you are now and accept the things about yourself that you cannot change, such as your height, your bone structure, and your general personality. Love yourself and your journey. Love your efforts, your accomplishments, and your failures. These are all the things that make you unique and special.

When you love yourself, you endeavor to take care of yourself physically, mentally, and emotionally. You take care to look and feel your best by nurturing your body, mind, and spirit.

Your challenge is to *do* something to nurture yourself and your love for yourself or simply, self-love. Some ideas:

- Exercise
- Eat healthy
- Meditate

- Pray
- Go to an art class or any class for fun
- Read
- Get a new hairstyle
- Get a massage
- Listen to or watch a motivational speaker
- Take a yoga class
- Meditate (again)
- Buy yourself a flower
- Take a walk in the park
- Get a facial or a spa treatment
- Visit a friend
- Write yourself a love note
- Watch your favorite movie
- Get a mani-pedi
- Take a bubble bath
- Sit in silence for ten minutes

Your relationship with yourself sets the tone for every other relationship that you have. (Robert Holden)

To your transformation!

SELF-LOVE #2

To love yourself right now, just as you are, is to give yourself heaven. Don't wait until you die. If you wait, you die now. If you love, you live now.

—Alan Cohen

Loving myself wasn't something I ever thought I was supposed to do. I thought that, if I loved myself, I was being self-centered and selfish, even narcissistic.

When I was growing up as the third child, the third daughter, I was teased by my older sister(s). I was called names like conceited, self-centered, and told that there were things about my body and facial structure that were unappealing and ugly. I developed an unnecessary concern over my appearance and was never satisfied with how I looked.

My father believed that children should be seen and not heard, so I learned to remain quiet and stifle my opinions. My thoughts or ideas were not valued. Therefore, I learned not to trust my own judgment.

There are multiple scenarios and reasons that we, as humans, develop our anxieties and fears. So, I am not saying that these two events alone are the precursors for my lack of self-love as an adult. However, these are two things in the journey of my life that did have an effect on me and on my ability to love myself.

I cannot change what happened in my past, but I can look at these occurrences, accept them for what they were, and move on with acceptance.

I can accept that I am reasonably attractive and of average intelligence. I can make changes by wearing makeup and wearing clothing that fits my body type. I can exercise to stay fit and healthy, if that's what I desire. I can take classes to improve my education and knowledge.

Loving myself is about accepting myself for who and what I am *now*. It's accepting what I cannot change about myself. And it's changing what I can to make myself the best version of myself that makes me happy to introduce myself to others.

To your transformation!

SELF-LOVE #3

You yourself, as much as anybody in the entire universe, deserve your love and affection.

—Buddha

There are so many famous and notable people throughout history who have quotes that reflect the importance of self-love that it's been quite difficult to choose which ones to use. However, it just proves the point that, though time may change, one thing remains constant. And that is the importance of loving yourself.

When you have self-love, you will have happiness in all other areas of your life.

Make a list of things that you love about yourself. Post the list where you can see it. Be grateful for the things that you love about yourself. Write a gratitude each day for yourself. (I am thankful for my intelligence. I am thankful for my kindness. I am thankful for my ability to solve problems. I am thankful for my patience. Write whatever you're grateful for.)

Accept yourself for where you are now. If you are having a "bad" day, accept it. Tomorrow is a new day. If you didn't do what you thought you "should" do today, accept it. Tomorrow is a new day. Accept yourself. Accept your feelings. Love yourself. Like the good and the not so good— together. The good and the not so good all make you special—uniquely *you*.

Do something every day that makes you happy. Be as loving to yourself as you would be to another person who you care about.

> Love yourself first and everything else falls into line. You really have to love yourself to get anything done in this world. (Lucille Ball)

To your transformation!

CHAPTER 64

SELF-RESPECT

SELF-RESPECT #1

Never violate the sacredness of your individual self-respect.
—Theodore Parker

In order to get respect from others, we must have respect for ourselves. But more than that, in order to get anything in life—including happiness and success—we must have self-respect.

Someone asked me, "What is the difference between self-confidence and self-respect?"

Self-confidence, by definition, is the ability to have faith in yourself to get the job done and do it well. Self-respect is to have morals and dignity and to feel good about yourself while you are doing your job well.

By definition, self-respect is a combination of self-confidence, pride, honor, and dignity in oneself. You continue to have regard for the position for which you take a stand and continue to stand up for yourself no matter what other people may think. You stand by your choices because you have faith in yourself and in your decisions.

You do the "right" thing, even when no one is watching! You respect yourself regardless of your past mistakes. You accept yourself the way you are even when other people may forsake you because *you* know that you are awesome.

Your challenge this week is to examine your level of self-respect. Do

240

you feel proud of yourself? Do you feel a sense of dignity in yourself and your behavior? Are you honored to, be you?

If you answered no to any of these questions, then ask yourself what you are doing to disrespect yourself. Do you want to change? Would you feel better with more self-respect? The abiding truth to that question is a resounding *yes*!

To your transformation!

> *Everyone in society can be a role model, not only for their own self-respect, but for respect from others.*
> —Unknown

SELF-RESPECT #2

> *It is the highest form of* self-respect *to admit our errors and mistakes and make amends for them. To make a mistake is only an error in judgment, but to adhere to it when it is discovered shows infirmity of character.*
> —Dale Turner

In order to make changes in your own self-respect, you need to admit your mistakes and move forward to better days. It's okay to make mistakes. We all make them! It doesn't make us bad or terrible people. It makes us human.

Accept yourself and admit your mistakes. Forgive yourself and move forward. (See "Forgiveness.")

Build your Self-Respect. Determine what you value and make a list. Write down steps for how you can achieve what you value (friendships, love, a home, a job, and so on).

Choose how you are going to think about your values. Be accountable. Be responsible. Write down ideas that you might have to get you to over come obstacles. Ask for help.

The willingness to accept responsibility for one's own life is the source from which self-respect springs. (Joan Didion)

Expect disappointments and setbacks.

When you know that you can overcome challenges, you do gain that self-respect, and then you won't end up in a situation that you regret later on. (Danica McKellar)

To your transformation!

SELF-RESPECT #3

Would that there were an award for people who come to understand the concept of enough. Good enough. Successful enough. Thin enough. Rich enough. Socially responsible enough. When you have self-respect, you have enough.
—Gail Sheehy

Self-respect is about satisfaction with who we are as a person—not striving for someone else's idea of who we ought to be.

So many of us, myself included, get caught up in society's ideas of perfection and absolutism. We believe that, if we aren't a certain height or weight, or if we don't make a certain amount of money or live in a certain location, we aren't successful, or we aren't good enough.

With self-respect, we don't need to fit a certain expectation set by others. We don't need to fit into a set pattern of behavior arranged by society. We simply need to respect ourselves "enough" to be happy and satisfied with our choices and to be proud of where we stand and proud of our accomplishments.

I WISH YOU ENOUGH

I wish you enough weakness so that you know the great measure of your strength.

I wish you enough sadness so that you learn to appreciate the moments of bliss.

I wish you enough joy so that you heart feels full and blessed.

I wish you enough hands to hold and lips to kiss so that you learn the meaning of love.

I wish you enough heartbreak so that you realize the true love you deserve.

I wish you enough loneliness so that you become independent and start loving yourself.

I wish you enough confidence so that you are capable but not conceited.

I wish you enough love so that you understand the meaning and significance of it and so that, when you're ready for it, you aren't scared to fall in.

I wish you enough laughter so that you learn to slow down and appreciate the people and things around you.

I wish you enough disappointment so that you never lose sight of all that you have.

I wish you enough pain so that you learn to stand on your own two feet and to trust God.

I wish you enough toughness to sustain through the hard days, and enough frailty to learn your own limits.

I wish you enough softness to forgive and enough resilience to begin again.

I wish you enough success so that you are proud of the skin you stand in.

I wish you enough loss so that you never take what you have for granted.

I wish you enough gain so that you are both humble and thankful.

I wish you enough stability so that you trust the world around you and the people in it but enough change so that you are always growing.

I wish you enough love, enough life, enough purpose, enough brokenness, enough wholeness so that your life is imperfect and beautiful and blessed.

I do not wish you flawlessness or perfection. I wish you a life worth living—a life with ups and downs, trials and triumphs, growth and beginnings and endings and lessons, and love.

I wish you enough.
Just enough.

To your transformation!

CHAPTER 65

SELF-TRUST

SELF-TRUST #1

Self-trust firms up your inner territory and grounds you with solid premises for believing in who you are.
—Laurie Nadel, *Dr. Laurie Nadel's Sixth Sense: Unlocking Your Ultimate Mind Power*

When you lack self-trust, you exhibit self-doubt and lack self-confidence.

Sometimes we hide behind our desire to look good in front of others, and we are afraid of making a mistake. We pretend that we know the right answers when, in fact, we do not.

I exhibited this behavior just this past week. Someone asked me a question, and I pretended that I knew the answer. So, I said, "Yes," when inside, I knew that the opposite was true. I knew that I was wrong—that I had made a mistake.

It wasn't a big thing; it was small. But I was afraid to show that I was fallible. Yet I was in a state of not trusting myself—not sure that I could be open and authentic in that moment with my truth.

When I realized that I had hidden my truth, I felt terribly broken and ashamed, which made it worse. In fact, my realization made me more authentic. I shared my truth with other people, family and friends who supported me with my personal growth.

Now I can learn not to doubt myself. Now that I know that I do this—not trust myself—I am able to trust myself in the future. Speak the truth. Don't be afraid to be vulnerable in front of others.

Your challenge this week: Stop seeking the advice of others and trust yourself and your own wisdom. The answers you seek lie within you.

To your transformation!

> *We have all a better guide in ourselves, if we would attend to it, than any other person can be.*
> —Jane Austen, *Mansfield Park*

SELF-TRUST #2

"As we learn to recognize and understand the body's subtle sensations, and then act on them, our self-trust will grow tremendously. To me it is rather amazing that the body has this innate sense of the truth, as if the body is hardwired for it," states psychotherapist John Prendergast, PhD.

Your mind, your heart and your body are all connected. If you find that you can't find the answers you seek in your mind, listen to your body.

There is an old saying that people use that says, "Follow your gut." Your body often gives you signals to let you know if something is right or wrong by how you feel. Your stomach might get upset. You might feel churning or tightness in your chest.

I had a younger colleague share with me recently that he "felt" like something was wrong in a dating relationship that he was having. He had a "feeling" in his being like there was a shift in the vibrations and signals being given out by the other person.

When you have those types of feelings or sense those changes, trust yourself! Trust your senses. If it feels wrong, it probably is wrong. If it feels right, it often is right.

Trust yourself.

To your transformation!

SELF-TRUST #3

Trust yourself. Create the kind of self that you will be happy to live with all your life. Make the most of yourself by fanning the tiny, inner sparks of possibility into flames of achievement.
—Golda Meir

So many of us, myself included, are stopped by fear. We are afraid to trust ourselves—afraid to trust our instincts.

We think of things that will make us happy. Yet we don't act on those thoughts because we think, *What if I'm wrong? What if I make the wrong decision?*

We then are immobilized, paralyzed, and stagnant. We continue that same old routine, stuck in the same place day after day, being unhappy.

How many times, as a kid, did you have a test in front of you and you were afraid to circle the answer on a multiple-choice test because you thought you didn't know the right answer? Time slipped by, and before you knew it, time was up, and the question went unanswered.

The trick is that you know more answers than you think. What would the answer be, if you *did* know the answer?

If you approach that test like you know the answers and make the best choice possible and leave nothing unanswered, you have the best chance of doing well on the test.

It's the same in life. You know the answers! You know what will make you happy. Make the choice.

Circle the answer. Go for it! Trust yourself.

You will feel your happiness quotient double, triple, and more, when you trust your instincts.

To your transformation!

As soon as you trust yourself, you will know how to live.
—Johann Wolfgang von Goethe, *Faust* (first part)

CHAPTER 66

SENSITIVITY

A sensitive soul sees the world through the lens of love.

—anonymous

There is so much talk about being sensitive in the world today. I hear it on the news almost every day. Yet do we really know what it means to be sensitive?

I consider myself a sensitive person, but what does that mean?

I have a big heart, which is open to *all* people without reservation. The beauty of the world continues to fill me with awe. Talents of artists move and inspire my soul. Animals and small creatures ignite the warmth of my spirit.

It has been said that sensitive people love more deeply and dream more vividly.[*] However, sensitive people also may suffer more intensely too.

> Sensitive people either love deeply or they regret deeply. There really is no middle ground because they live in passionate extremes. (Shannon L. Alder)

It is important to recognize your own level of sensitivity.

---

[*] Dreaming is not necessarily at night while you are sleeping but may be during a wakeful moment as in a daydream.

Your challenge this week is to think about your personality and your nature of sensitivity.

Follow these next steps if you're holding onto regret or dwelling in the past:

- Learn to let it go! Make a conscious decision to let whatever it is that has been bothering you *go, go, go*!
- Express your pain. Either talk to someone about it, record yourself, or write in a journal
- Take responsibility for what happened!
- *Stop* blaming others! Stop being a victim!
- Enjoy your life *now*! Be in *this* moment! Find something to be grateful for now!
- Forgive the other person or persons! Forgive *yourself*!
- Continue to be sensitive and live deeply and fully now!

To your transformation!

SENSITIVITY #2

> *Never apologize for being* sensitive *or emotional. It's a sign that you have a big heart, and that you aren't afraid to let others see it. Showing your emotions is a sign of strength.*
> —Brigitte Nicole

I cry easily. I cry often.

Sometimes when I have the television on, I might see something that touches my emotions and it brings a lump in my throat or a tear to my eye. It can even be something as simple as a picture on a commercial.

Now, does that mean I'm a sap? A weakling? A baby?

No! I'm just sensitive. And that's all right! It's a strength really. Being sensitive lets other people know who you are from the very beginning of any relationship.

I am sure you have heard the phrase, "wearing one's heart on one's sleeve." This describes a person whose feelings and emotions are out in the open for everyone to see.

Being sensitive can sometimes be a problem however, if/when, a person becomes immobilized by their sensitivity. If, we become afraid of other people's reactions to us or overly sensitive to what people think of us and, therefore, we do not want to go out, we can be overcome with anxiety. And that is *not* a good thing.

Sensitive people sometimes become overwrought with anxiety and depression due to outside circumstances, rejection, and criticism. The trick is to learn to handle it by accepting it.

> Rather than fearfully shutting down your sensitivity, dive in deeper into all possible feeling. (Victoria Erickson)

Understanding yourself and others is a key to accepting yourself and your sensitivity *and* accepting others.

To your transformation!

SENSITIVITY #3

> *Why is* sensitivity *perceived as being dangerous? When we're sensitive, we feel things we were taught not to feel. When we're sensitive, we are completely open to attack. When we're sensitive, we are awake and in touch with our hearts—and this can be very threatening to the status quo indeed.*
> —Aletheia Luna, *Awakened Empath: The Ultimate Guide to Emotional, Psychological and Spiritual Healing*

Being sensitive is not just about being in touch with our own hearts and our own emotions.

Sensitivity also includes reaching out to others and the ability to recognize what another person needs, sometimes without asking. It's an awareness of other people's rights, their physical and personal space, and their overall emotional state.

While some people have a more intuitive sense of the needs of another, there are many folks who fall short of this mark.

Therefore, a booming new industry of sensitivity training has been developed for those who need assistance.

I would venture to guess that a large majority of our population would benefit from sensitivity training.

After all, half of the world is male, who would benefit from understanding females. And the other half of the world is female, who would benefit from understanding males. Neither of us really knows what it's like living in the skin of the opposite gender—not to mention all of the other gender, race, class, ethnic, and other issues that we would all benefit from understanding and having sensitivity for.

Everyone can start by using good manners in *all* situations.

> Manners are a *sensitive* awareness of the feelings of others.
> If you have that awareness, you have good manners, no matter what fork you use. (Emily Post)

It's a beginning! Then start by looking up sensitivity training online.

We are all human beings regardless of gender, race, class, ethnicity, or creed. If we can remember to treat one another like human beings in kind, it will be a great beginning.

To your transformation!

CHAPTER 67

STRENGTH

STRENGTH #1

You have power over your mind—not outside events. Realize this, and you will find strength. —Marcus Aurelius

A younger friend of mine told me that he had control over his abusive behavior toward others, as long as life did not throw him any events that he could not easily handle.

Hmmmmmm. I question. Is that controlling your life or is life controlling you? Are you cultivating your strength? Are you managing your life so that it works for you?

First, what does it mean to have inner strength?

It means you are strong both emotionally and psychologically and can confront difficulties of all kinds—no matter what challenges life might throw your way. You have energy and stamina to problem solve when facing a challenge. You are not only able to think it through but also able to take action. And by action, I do not mean abusive action! Action taken would be solving your problems in positive ways. And if you don't know how to solve the problem, you seek help from others who do.

Second, how do you cultivate inner strength?

It's important to learn how to calm yourself. Learn how to de-stress at the end of the day and during the day. Listen to music that calms your soul. Take a break. Take a walk outside. Take a bath with soothing oils.

Sit in silence for ten minutes to regroup. Meditate! Create a nurturing home environment for yourself. Make your home a place where you feel safe and warm.

Home should be a refuge and a comforting place to be, where you can recharge yourself. Surround yourself at home with things you love. Home should be a healthy and inviting place that you want to go to at the end of the day.

Surround yourself with positive, productive, and supportive people. Productive people get the job done! They take action and will support you in your action! Distance yourself from complainers and negative behavior.

Cultivate physical strength through exercise! When your inner strength wanes, you will find that you will be able to rely on your physical strength to carry you through with action during the tough times.

Read motivational material (books, articles, blogs, and the like). Watch motivational videos on YouTube, TV, or the web in general. Mindless TV is a waste of time and a waste of energy. Watch one motivational speaker or read one motivational article per day. Or listen to one motivational song to get you going in the morning! "Stronger" by Kelly Clarkson is a good one.

Forgive yourself! You aren't going to be able to be perfect in maintaining inner strength in all situations every day. Forgive yourself your shortcomings and move forward one day at a time. The more you practice having strength, the stronger you will become.

Celebrate your successes! Call a friend and let him or her know about each obstacle that you have overcome, no matter how small. Cheer your success together. Bake a cake and blow out the candle. Smile a *lot*! Be happy. You are winning at life.

Your challenge this week is to cultivate your inner strength *and* to share with another person what you are doing to make yourself stronger on the inside.

To your transformation!

No matter what kind of challenges or difficulties or painful situations you go through in your life, we all have something deep within us that we can reach down and find the inner strength to get through them. —Alana Stewart

STRENGTH #2

Few men during their lifetime come anywhere near exhausting the resources dwelling within them. There are deep wells of strength that are never used.

—*Richard E. Byrd*

We all have within us, whether we are aware of them or not, a reserve of natural strengths. Our natural strengths make up a large part of our character and help define who we are as a person. These natural strengths include but are not limited to traits such as:

- Bravery
- Curiosity
- Creativity
- Fairness
- Forgiveness
- Honesty
- Humor
- Humility
- Good judgment
- Kindness
- Leadership
- Love
- Sincerity
- Trustworthiness

Many of the characteristics that I have written about in this book are examples of natural strengths.

Unfortunately, we get caught up in the negative and often dwell in the criticisms of our personalities and focus on our weaknesses. In order to build inner strength, we *must* dwell on our natural strengths.

Take a moment or ten minutes and make a list of at least five (but it can be more) of your own personal natural strengths.

Take your list and post it in a place in your home, your refuge, where you can see it every day—and remind yourself that you are strong and you have these wonderful, powerful, strong natural resources inside of yourself to help you when you need strength.

This is the core of your inner strength. Make your list. Post your list.

To your transformation!

STRENGTH #3

> *You never know how strong you are until being strong is the only choice you have.*
>
> —Bob Marley

Sometimes you don't figure out how strong you are until there is a crisis and you step up to help, without even thinking about the consequences to yourself.

Or you figure out how strong you really are when you have to take care of another person, and you are responsible for the life of that other person.

Whatever the circumstance, strength comes forward without conscious thought. Your inner reserve of strength simply takes over and goes into action to get the job done—whatever job that needs to be done in order to ensure the safety and well-being of those in your care.

Treat yourself as if you were in your own care! Step up with strength and take the action necessary to build your best life—one day at a time.

You need only to answer to yourself each day with grace and forgiveness.

> A truly strong person does not need the approval of others any more than a lion needs the approval of sheep. (Vernon Howard)

To your transformation!

CHAPTER 68

TRANSITION

Change is situational. Transition, on the other hand, is psychological. *It is not those events but, rather, the inner reorientation or self-redefinition that you have to go through in order to incorporate any of those changes into your life. Without a transition, a change is just a rearrangement of the furniture. Unless transition happens, the change won't work, because it doesn't take.*

—*William Bridges*

By definition, transition is the process of changing from one state to another. Therefore, transition does not happen in a moment or even a day. It may take many moments or many days for the process to become complete.

Life is a series of transitions.

Upon the completion of one transition, you may be headed into a new transition and the beginning of a new process or journey.

We transition from the womb to life outside of the womb to life as a child to living our lives as independent adults, with many steps/transitions prior to that along the way.

As we grow and mature, our lives are a series of transitions from one developmental level to the next. Some of us take more time to process each transition.

Transitions are challenging, confusing, and laden with fear. It is our mission and your challenge to recognize your newest transition—the one that is waiting around the corner, the one you are afraid to begin—and take a small step toward that process of change.

Every new event in our life is a transition. A new friend is a transition. A new job is a transition. And so is a new living arrangement, a new car, a new relationship, or a breakup.

Even going on a vacation is a transition as you adjust to a new environment, new foods, new schedule, new climate, and so on.

Coming home from a vacation is also a transition as you adjust back into your routine and regular way of life.

You transition from one way of being to another way of being.

> A lot of people resist transition and therefore never allow themselves to enjoy who they are. Embrace the change, no matter what it is; once you do, you can learn about the new world you're in and take advantage of it. (Nikki Giovanni)

To your transformation!

TRANSITION #2

> *Times of* transition *are strenuous, but I love them. They are an opportunity to purge, rethink priorities, and be intentional about new habits. We can make our new normal any way we want*
>
> —Kristin Armstrong

When you are in the process of transition, you need to give yourself time, *because transition is not easy. But you have the opportunity to make your transitions positive.*

Allow time for your mind to absorb the effects of the changes on your life. Reflect on the learning that this change brings you. What is the lesson? There is a lesson in every event in our life. Look for the positive that this transition can provide.

How will life be different as you transition from one "place" to the other (place may be literal or figurative).

Recently, I was on a trip abroad for the first time. I was alone without family or close friends, which caused anxiety and fear. Being in a strange land, I found that a different culture was both exciting and intimidating. I was forced to look for the good, the wonder, and the possibility in spite of my fear.

Give yourself permission to move forward, to look ahead to brighter futures.

> Any *transition* is easier if you believe in yourself and your talent. (Priyanka Chopra)

Look for the benefits that transition will bring. Make a list of positive attributes.

Make the changes that make you the happiest. Your time is now.

To your transformation!

TRANSITION #3

> *Light precedes every transition. Whether at the end of a tunnel, through a crack in the door or the flash of an idea, it is always there, heralding a new beginning.*
> —Teresa Tsalaky

As an adult, young, old, or in between, you generally get an inkling or a sense that something is not exactly right or something needs to change.

Sometimes you get a twinkling of an idea in your mind, a brief thought or flash of what we call an "aha moment."

That is the light. That is the sense that you need to heed. It is calling you into a transition!

Sometimes we don't act on our sense because we are afraid. We're afraid to change because change, no matter what it is, is hard. *But* your life does not get better by chance. It gets better by change.

> Transitions themselves are not the issue, but how well you respond to their challenges! (Jim George)

Be the change you want to see in yourself. And then, you can be the change you want to see in the world!

To your transformation!

CHAPTER 69

VALUES

VALUES #1

Your beliefs become your thoughts,
Your thoughts become your words,
Your words become your actions,
Your actions become your habits,
Your habits become your values,
Your values *become your destiny.*

—Mahatma Gandhi

Why do we do the things we do? Our actions are based, for the most part, on what we care about, which is based on our values.

Generally, we get our values from our parents and from the environment in which we are raised.

We choose to keep the values that we agree with and change the values that we disagree with based on our individual personality, societal influences, and economic influences.

Our values can change as we change throughout our life.

Therefore, it is important to identify what you value, reevaluating from time to time. What makes you happy? What makes you unhappy? Live your life accordingly.

Your challenge is to identify your values.

Living your values will bring you happiness.

To your transformation!

VALUES #2

> *It's not hard to make decisions when you know what your values are.*
>
> —Roy Disney

When you know yourself, you understand who you are by recognizing what you value.

If I value cleanliness, I will keep a clean home and clean personal space.

If I value truth, I will be honest and forthcoming in what I do.

If I value having "fine" possessions, I will earn the money to buy those possessions.

If I value knowledge, I will pursue an education.

And the list goes on. I am sure you get the idea of defining who you are by your values. Doing so makes it easier to stand up for yourself in all situations. It also makes it easier to stand up for others who struggle to have a voice of their own.

When you value justice, you will not stand by in silence and allow injustice to occur to yourself or others.

Whether it is in your personal life or in business, decision making is matched through your value system. That's why, when you work for a company, it's important to work for one whose value system matches your own.

An honest person will not last long in a company that is not forthcoming and honest with its customers. The decision making of the honest employee will not suit the decision making of the company policy.

You are a better person and a better leader when you lead from your values.

Continue to understand yourself by identifying your values.

To your transformation!

VALUES #3

Never compromise your values.
—Steve Maraboli, *Life, the Truth, and Being Free*

Only you know what your values are. Only you know what is important to you.

If you compromise your values, you will find that you will have internal struggles. These struggles may manifest themselves as anger, frustration, depression, anxiety, or other sorts of negative emotions that do not belong to the positive human being that you deserve to be.

When you experience any of the above negative emotions, examine your values and ask yourself, are one or more of my values being compromised?

Evaluate your situation.

Make changes accordingly to be true to your value system, and happiness will follow.

Sometimes it takes time to make the changes necessary.

Sometimes it takes courage.

You *can* do this! Align yourself with your values.

To your transformation!

CHAPTER 70

WELLNESS

Wellness is the complete integration of body, mind, and spirit—the realization that everything we do, think, feel, and believe has an effect on our state of well-being. —Greg Anderson

There are so many aspects of wellness—all integrated into one which equals ourselves. We cannot focus on being well in only one area of our lives and say that we are "healthy," because each and every area of our body, mind, and spirit has a significant effect and impact on the other.

We go to the gym and eat "right" and struggle to lose weight so that we can "be healthy."

We make doctor appointments and go to the dentist and go to yoga so that we can live healthfully.

We go to church or temple or pray so our spirits can thrive and be healthy.

We clean our home and wash our cars and take a shower so that we can look healthy.

We buy new clothes and cut our hair and wear makeup, so we appear healthy.

Are we healthy? Are we thinking healthfully? How uncluttered are our minds? How are we creating mental and emotional health? For ourselves? for others?

Your challenge this week is to check in with yourself and your wellness—your mental and emotional wellness. Check on the mental and emotional wellness of your friends and family and others that you encounter—your coworkers, neighbors, and the people you meet.

Tell people that they matter. Tell them that you love them—that you care and that they make a difference in your life and in the lives of others every day. Acknowledge everyone for the work that they do. Acknowledge even the simplest acts and tasks.

Your kindness makes a difference!

Live for today. Do not stress about what may have happened yesterday or last year. Do not worry about tomorrow. Live in the present moment and be grateful for today.

> The secret of health for both mind and body is not to mourn for the past, not to worry about the future, or not to anticipate troubles, but to live in the present moment wisely and earnestly. (Buddha)

To your transformation!

WELLNESS #2

> *The concept of total wellness recognizes that our every thought, word, and behavior affect our greater health and well-being. And we, in turn, are affected not only emotionally but also physically and spiritually.*
> —Greg Anderson

When we have negative thoughts about ourselves or when we get stuck in thoughts that we cannot move past—like old stories of ourselves and how other people expect us to act—we create stress and get physically ill.

However, we may not even be aware that we are doing this to ourselves. Sometimes we need to *stop* and take a look at our life and examine ourselves and whether or not we are happy with what we are doing.

Are we living our life for ourselves or are we living according to the plan that others have laid out for us? Sometimes we just go with the easier path, because it's there, in front of us. We don't question it. But we aren't happy with that path, and we get stressed and sick, either emotionally or physically.

Perhaps we were rude to the person in line in front of us at the store yesterday. Maybe we yelled at our kids or snapped at our significant other for no apparent reason. We get physically and emotionally sick over our lack of compassion and love for others and for ourselves. Our unhappiness shows up in many different ways throughout the course of a day. Sometimes we feel sad or start to cry, but we cannot figure out why.

The first step to *stop* the unhappiness is to *take action*! Examine your path. Check your happiness quotient. Maybe it's time to make a change.

Go for a walk. Exercise. Move your body. Get outside. If you can't get outside, do stretches inside your house to start.

Just move!

When you move and exercise your body, your brain release endorphins, which will elevate your mood and help you to think more clearly. It will help you to feel better/happier about yourself.

When we are happy, we are able to share our love and our joy more easily. It comes more naturally because we have it more readily available to share.

Moving your body may be the first step in a list of changes you may want to make. Change can be frightening, so reach out to friends and family for support. Join a group. Email me.

We *are all* in this world together—with love.

To your transformation!

WELLNESS #3

> *In a disordered mind, as in a disordered body, soundness of health is impossible.*
> —Marcus Tullius Cicero

When you have something on your mind and you are stopped by whatever it is that is filling your thoughts, you need to get it out of your head so that you can move forward and be *well*.

One of the best ways to clear your mind is to share what you are thinking and going through with another person. However, that is not always an easy task.

We may get into a conversation with a family member or with a friend but how do we open the subject that we really want to talk about? Do we just blurt it out? Do we simply say, "I need to talk"?

It's not that easy for many people. And, therefore, so many of us just hold all of our thoughts and feeling inside. We harbor our thoughts until it feels so overwhelming, and we don't know what to do or how to handle it.

Here are some ways to make it easier to share your inner most thoughts with another person:

- Choose someone with whom you feel comfortable. It could be a family member, a friend, a clergy member, a teacher, a coworker, or anyone else you feel comfortable with. Comfort and personal safety are important.
- Simply start the conversation with, "Do you have time to talk?" or, "I could use an ear to bounce some thoughts off of. Are you up for that?
- If you get together, you can start with small talk. Ask if the other person would be open to listening to what you have been going through. For example, you might say, "I have been struggling with _____ lately. And it has been very difficult for me."

If you have the right person, your listener will ask you questions about your experience to help you sort out your thoughts and to help you share. Sometimes you get the wrong person and get "shut down" because the listener is not able to step outside of his or her own thoughts to listen to yours. Try not to get discouraged. Just choose a different person to talk with. Not everyone is a good listener.

To be healthy as a whole, Mental wellness plays a role.
(author unknown)

Keep looking for your listeners. They are out there, and you must be able to clear your mind.

(Licensed counselors and therapists are available for in-person talk therapy. Ask you family doctor for referrals or check online for your insurance coverage. Some talk therapy is available via computer and/or telephone. Life coaches are available through social media referrals. Just be sure to verify licensing and certifications before payment of services.)

Other methods for mind clearing are meditation, yoga, listening to music, exercise, artistic activities, journaling, running, or spending time in nature.

To your wellness and *to your transformation!*

CHAPTER 71

WORRY

Worry does not empty tomorrow of its sorrow; it empties today of its strength.

—*Corrie ten Boom*

Worry seems to be coming up a lot lately. In my life and in the lives of the people around me, everyone seems to be worried about something or someone.

First let me say that there is a distinct difference between worry and concern. As a wife, mother, and friend, I am always concerned about the welfare of the people in my life. When there is a problem, a concerned person steps up with a solution. If we cannot offer a solution, then at least we can offer some brainstorming toward a solution.

When our children are very young, we don't sit around worrying about things like, "How will they ever manage in this world?" We step up with solutions and teach them to problem solve. We teach our children to become competent adults.

When they are finally adults, it comes down to faith. You have faith that you did your job as a parent. You have faith that your children *are* competent adults, good citizens, and intelligent and happy people who can solve problems. And finally, you have faith in your higher power that they are protected by God and that whatever is going to happen will happen.

Your challenge this week is to stop worrying. Take action to solve problems. Make changes. And find peace in having faith that God will provide the way.

To your transformation!

> *There is only one way to happiness and that is to cease worrying about things which are beyond the power of our will.*
>
> —Epictetus

WORRY #2

> *If a problem is fixable, if a situation is such that you can do something about it, then there is no need to worry. If it's not fixable, then there is no help in worrying. There is no benefit in worrying whatsoever.*
>
> —Dalai Lama XIV

No worry? That's great, right?

But how do you stop worrying when it is all you have ever done and all you know how to do?

First, make a list of what you worry about. Write all things down even the smallest things. Write down the people you worry about.

Second, look at your list and separate the list into two categories— things you *can* do something about and things you *cannot* do anything about.

List number one contains problems you can solve. Take action on this list—one at a time—without worry.

- Examples include:
- Pay the bills.
- Get help with the housework.
- Look for a job.
- Make a doctor's appointment.

Take *action* on those things, one action at a time.

List number two contains problems you cannot solve. These may include things like another person's financial problems (you can give moral support however), world peace (you can join an organization to provide support) or world hunger (feed the homeless at a food pantry or otherwise volunteer).

If there are things that you worry about that you simply cannot control, like gun violence for example, and you cannot think of a way to offer community service, meditate or pray.

This is where faith comes into your life. Have faith that you can give to your higher power that which is His or Hers to control.

> How would your life be different if ...? You stopped worrying about things you can't control and started focusing on the things you can? Let today be the day ... You free yourself from fruitless worry, seize the day and take effective action on things you can change. (Steve Maraboli, *Life, the Truth, and Being Free*)

To your transformation!

WORRY #3

> *If you believe that feeling bad or worrying long enough will change a past or future event, then you are residing on another planet with a different reality system.*
> —William James

No one can change the past.

Whatever happened happened. We can take our lessons from the people and events of our past and move forward.

Our past is what makes us who we are today. And if we learn along the way, it helps shape who we are.

If we spend time worrying about our future, then we create anxiety and stress for ourselves—instead of enjoying our present. We agonize over past decisions, whether or not they were the right ones or the wrong ones.

Did I make the best choice?

Could I have done better?

Should I have gone in another direction with my life?

There is no such thing as a good or bad decision. (I am not talking about deliberately hurting yourself or another, of course; that is not a good decision.)

I'm talking about decisions like which job to take, which house to rent/buy, which person to date, and the like. They are all just decisions that we made at the time—based on the information that we had in the moment.

Take the time you need to make the best decisions you can by looking at all the information you have—intellectual data, emotional instinct, physical logistics. Take *all* of your information into account.

Decide and move forward.

Be open and honest with yourself and others along the way.

Stop worrying about it. If you determine that you don't like your decision down the road, then you can make a new decision to move in a new direction.

Life is full of new opportunities every day. Take action and enjoy it. Try to have some fun along the way.

> It is difficult to live in and enjoy the moment when you are thinking about the past or worrying about the future. You cannot change your past, but you can ruin the present by worrying about your future. Learn from the past, plan for the future. The more you live in and enjoy the present moment, the happier you will be.
>
> (Roy T. Bennett, *The Light in the Heart*)

To your transformation!

RESOURCES

Aron, Arthur. "The Experimental Generation of Interpersonal Closeness." *Personality and Social Psychology Bulletin*, NY (April 1997) V.23 Issue 4 pg. 363-377

Austin, Michael W., PhD. "Achieving Happiness Advice from Plato," *Psychology Today* (2010). https://www.psychologytoday.com/us/blog/ethics-everyone/201008/achieving-happiness-advice-plato.

Brenner, Abigail, MD. "Five Benefits of Stepping out of Your Comfort Zone." Posted 12/5/2015 verified by *Psychology Today*. https://www.psychologytoday.com/us/blog/in-flux/201512/5-benefits-stepping-outside-your-comfort-zone.

B. Zoe, - life and career coach - https://simplelifestrategies.com/sls-personal-values-successful-living/2012

Calvert, Drew. "5 Tips to Become an Authentic Leader." *Kellogg Insight* (March 7, 2016). https://insight.kellogg.northwestern.edu/article/five-tips-for-authentic-leadership

Caramela, Sammi. "The Management Theory of Frank and Lillian Gilbreth." (February 2018). https://www.business.com/articles/management-theory-of-frank-and-lillian-gilbreth/.

Cherry, Kendra, "Can People Learn to Be More Compassionate? Research Suggests the Brain Can Be Trained in Compassion." (April 21,

2019). https://www.verywellmind.com/can-people-learn-to-be-more-compassionate-2795560

Clear, James. "How long Does it Actually Take to Form a New Habit? (Backed by Science)." Behavioral Psychology, Habits. https://jamesclear.com/new-habit

Collins Dictionary. "Decency." (2010) Harpers Collins Publishers 4th edition https://www.collinsdictionary.com/us/dictionary/english/decency

Connolly, Michele. "On Happiness—Socrates." (2007). https://www.happinessstrategies.com/2007/09/08/on-happiness-socrates/

Conservapedia. "The Efficiency Movement." 2009. https://www.conservapedia.com/Efficiency_Movement.

Datson, Susan, PhD, director of Psychosocial and Spiritual Care. "Tips for Reducing Stress." *Cornerstone Hospice & Palliative Care* (2019). https://web.cshospice.org/feeling-stressed/.

Dyer, Wayne W. *Erroneous Zones*. Harper Collins, 1976. *Change Your Thoughts Change Your Life: The Wisdom of the Tao.* Hay House, 2007.

Economy, Peter, The Leadership Guy, "7 Keys to Becoming a Remarkably Effective Leader." *Inc.* (2016). https://www.inc.com/peter-economy/7-keys-becoming-effective-manager.html.

Fallon, Allison. "Why It's So Hard to Love Yourself and How It Can Change Your Life, "love-yourself. February 2016 https://allisonfallon.com/love-yourself/

Gibran, Kahlil. *The Prophet*. Knopf Doubleday Publishing Group, 1923.

Gillihan, Seth J., PhD. "Do People Really Change?" *Psychology Today* (2017). https://www.psychologytoday.com/us/blog/think-act-be/201701/do-people-really-change

Gladwell, Malcolm. *Blink: The Power of Thinking Without Thinking.* New York: Back Bay Books Little, Brown and Co., Hachette Book Co, NY10104, 2005.

Horstman, Mark. "The Effective Manager: The How to Guide for Effective Management." February 23, 2018.

Itani, Mustapha. "Aristotle on Friendship." (2017). https://medium.com/@mustaphahitani/aristotle-on-friendship-4384a899d647

Kruger, Kathy. "How to Balance Yin and Yang in Your Life and Yoga Practice." https://www.doyouyoga.com/how-to-balance-yin-and-yang-in-your-life-and-yoga-practice-57241/.

Liddle, Sarah. "40 Self-Care Techniques to Rejuvenate and restore Yourself." *Lifehack.* (2018) https://www.lifehack.org/364592/40-self-care-techniques-rejuvenate-and-restore-yourself.

Llopis, Glenn. "Five Ways Leaders Must Build a Family Environment to Achieve Excellence. *Forbes* (2012). https://www.forbes.com/sites/glennllopis/2012/08/13/5-ways-leaders-must-build-a-family-environment-to-achieve-excellence/#56ef7cf17247.

Loehr, Anne. "How to Live with Purpose Identify your Values and Improve your Leadership." Huffington Post US edition (5/2014 - 6:21pmET-updated 2017). https://www.huffpost.com/entry/how-to-live-with-purpose-_b_5187572

McGuire, Jane. "Beginner's Marathon Training Plan." *Runner's World Magazine* (2019). https://www.runnersworld.com/uk/training/marathon/a776459/marathon-training-plans/.

McLeod, Saul. "Maslow's Hierarchy of Needs." *Simply Psychology* (2018). https://www.simplypsychology.org/maslow.html.

Pendergrass, Kimberly, "Ten Positive Body Language Techniques to Help You Succeed." (2013). https://blog.udemy.com/positive-body-language/

Reid, Tori. "Improve your Relationships by Working on Yourself First." *Lifehacker* (2014). https://lifehacker.com/improve-your-relationships-by-working-on-yourself-first-1639053602.

Ribanszki, Robert, Psychology of Expectations. Sept. 12, 2019. Thrive Therapeutic Limited. https://thrive.uk.com/whatwedo.html.

Robinson, Lawrence; R. Segal, MA; J, Segal, PhD; and M. Smith M, MA. "Relaxation Techniques for Stress Relief," *Help Guide* (June 2019). https://www.helpguide.org/articles/stress/relaxation-techniques-for-stress-relief.htm

Saunderson, Roy. "Giving the Real Recognition," London Ontario-based (2008). https://c.ymcdn.com/sites/recognition.site-ym.com/resource/resmgr/imported/ArticleDoYouEvenKnowMe1.pdf.

Setton Mark K. & Phil, D., CEO & Founder, The Pursuit of Happiness https://www.pursuit-of-happiness.org/history-of-happiness/aristotle/

Stream, Carol. Illinois, 60188. All rights reserved. Ecclesiastes 11:4 in all English translations. The Living Bible. Tyndale House Foundation, 1971. Used by permission of Tyndale House Publishers Inc.,

Tang, Ian. "Three Kinds of Friends you Meet in Life." (2015). https://medium.com/@iantang/3-kinds-of-friends-you-meet-in-life-6b03c8383a85.

Taylor, Jim PhD, The Power of Prime: Personal Growth: Your Values, Your Life. (May 2012). https://www.psychologytoday.com/us/blog/the-power-prime/201205/personal-growth-your-values-your-life

Thompson, Kevin. "Two Words that Define Good Leadership." (2013). https://www.kevinathompson.com/i-love-people-who-have-this/.

Thorp, Tris, - Vedic Educator, What Your Values Can Teach You. (10/27/16) The Chopra Center. https://chopra.com/articles/what-your-values-can-teach-you

Tolle, Eckhart. *The Power of Now: A Guide to Spiritual Enlightenment.* Namaste Publishing, 1997; New World Library, 1999.

Ury, William. *The Power of a Positive NO: How to Say No and Still get to Yes.* New York: Bantam Dell, Division of Random House Inc., 2007.

Williams, Margery. *The Velveteen Rabbit.* 1922.

Printed in the United States
By Bookmasters